Books by Pauline Chatterton

Crochet: Fashion and Furnishings
The Art of Crochet
Patchwork and Appliqué
Scandinavian Knitting Designs
Coordinated Crafts for the Home

COORDINATED

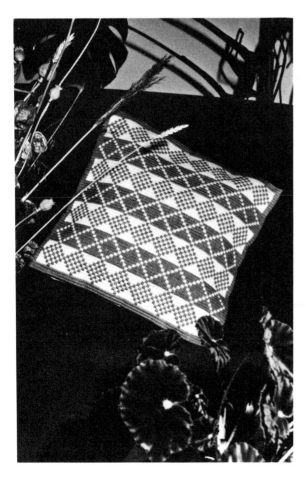

Pauline Chatterton

CRAFTS FOR THE HOME

Richard Marek Publishers • NEW YORK

Library of Congress Cataloging in Publication Data

Chatterton, Pauline.

  Coordinated crafts for the home.

  1. Textile crafts. I. Title.

TT699.C43   746.4   79-22244

ISBN 0-399-90060-8

Printed in the United States of America

Design by Lynn Braswell

Figure calligraphy by Sandra Brawarsky

Contents

3 · *Patchwork Designs*   *121*

Color plates follow page 96

Introduction

It is the aim of this book to provide some easy-to-make, but interesting, coordinated looks for interior design in the home, using a basic knowledge of such crafts as knitting, crochet, canvas embroidery, and latch-hook rug-making. It is to be hoped that the book will be a working handbook for people who want to create distinctive and subtly blended interiors through the skill of their own hands. Different members of one family may well be able to contribute their varied craft skills to the same project.

The design areas I have chosen to work in are Scandinavian, Patchwork, and African, all themes of some importance for crafts in America today. The Scandinavian and Patchwork designs provide a sound traditional element, while the African projects add an interesting new look.

Although it is assumed that the reader will have a basic working knowledge of the crafts in question, Chapter 1 gives useful hints on how to finish the work professionally, and also provides instructions for any unusual techniques or stitches used in the book. It is very important to read through this chapter carefully before you begin working any of the projects which follow.

1 . Instructions, Hints, and Guidelines

Each of the designs in this book is graded, according to the degree of difficulty, by the following simple star system:

* means the project is very simple to make;

** means that the project is a little more complicated, but can be easily worked by someone with patience and concentration who has already successfully tackled a similar project;

*** means the project should not be worked by anyone who has not had considerable previous experience in working in this particular craft field.

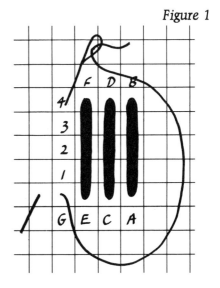

Figure 1

STITCHES USED FOR CANVAS WORK

UPRIGHT GOBELIN STITCH

Figure 1 shows the method for working Upright Gobelin Stitch over 4 meshes of the canvas. It is basically the same stitch used in Bargello or Florentine work, and anyone familiar with that stitch will be able to work any of the projects in this book. The stitches may be worked from right to left (as shown) or from left to right. Remember to begin working the charts at the bottom left-hand corner if you are more used to working in that direction.

Figure 2 shows how a second row of stitches is worked above the first. The charts given for the projects are easy to follow.

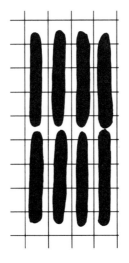

top of one row and lower edge of next are in the same mesh

Figure 2

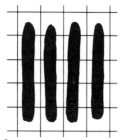

Figure 3

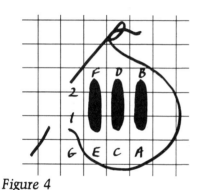

Figure 4

One square on the graph generally equals 4 stitches and 4 meshes on the canvas, unless otherwise indicated. Each square on the chart equals 1 "block" of 4 stitches worked over 4 meshes of the canvas, as shown in Figure 3.

Figure 4 shows the method for working Upright Gobelin Stitch over 2 meshes of the canvas. It is the same Straight Stitch used for working over 4 meshes, but is exactly half the length. This shorter stitch gives a much finer and more detailed look to the finished canvas, coming close to traditional needlepoint in delicacy, without the attendant problems of being slow to work and distorting the canvas.

Figure 5 shows how a second row of stitches is worked above the first.

When this stitch is used, 1 square on the chart equals 2 stitches and 2 meshes on the canvas, that is, a "block" of 2 stitches worked over 2 meshes of the canvas as shown in Figure 6. The same stitch may also be worked over 6 meshes of the canvas as shown in Figure 7.

When working any straight stitches, it is a good idea to let the yarn hang free of the canvas from time to time, as it has a tendency to wind up during work. Letting the strand unwind from time to time will help to keep the yarn flat and full on the canvas, and give you much better coverage.

Any of the designs in this book can be worked in more traditional needlepoint stitches, such as the Continental and Half

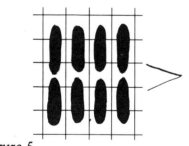

Figure 5

top of one row
and lower edge of
next are in the
same mesh

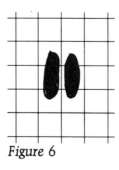

Figure 6

Figure 7

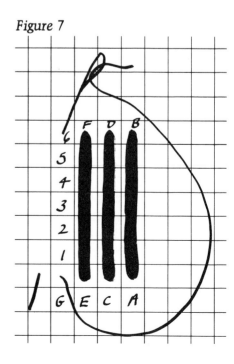

Cross. You will have to interpret each square on the chart accordingly, 4 × 4 stitches or 2 × 2 stitches, as the case may be. You may need slightly more yarn, and you will certainly have to block the finished canvas to counteract distortion through working a Diagonal Stitch.

DIAGONAL STITCH WORKED ON PLASTIC CANVAS

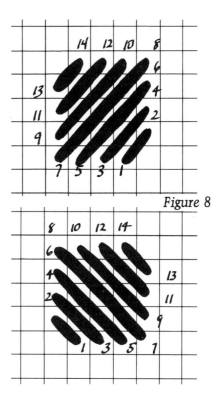

Figure 8

When working on plastic canvas with 7 holes to 1″, and using a Persian or 4-ply yarn, a Straight Stitch will not cover at all well. I have, therefore, developed a simple Diagonal Stitch which is worked in squares or "blocks." It covers the canvas very quickly and, because the plastic is rigid, the troublesome distortion normally associated with diagonal stitches doesn't apply.

Figure 8 shows how the stitch is worked. It does not matter in which direction you choose to work the slanting stitches, provided you remember to keep all the stitches running in the same direction.

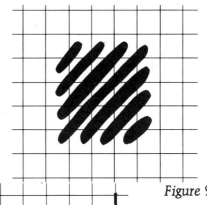

Figure 9 shows a completed "block" of stitches, which is equivalent to 1 square on the charts provided in subsequent chapters for working on plastic canvas.

Figure 10 shows how the blocks are worked side by side and row on top of row.

Figure 11 shows how you should begin working the stitch, as close as possible to the edges of the plastic canvas. This will save time in trimming the canvas when the work is completed.

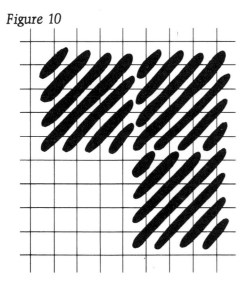

Figure 10

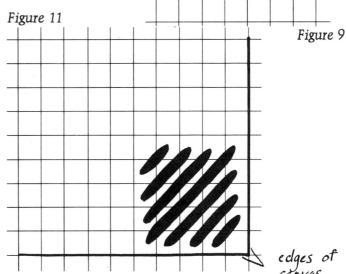

Figure 11

Figure 9

edges of canvas

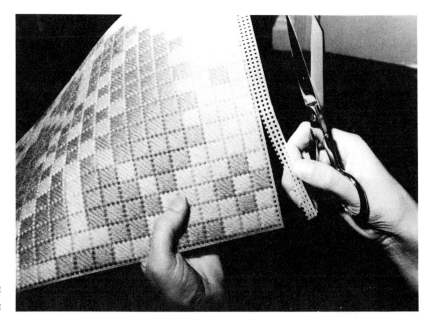

Photo 1: *Trimming Excess*
Canvas

Photograph 1 shows how the excess canvas is trimmed away when work is complete. Make sure that you cut as close as you can to the cross "threads" of the canvas; otherwise you will have unattractive little "teeth" of plastic showing along the edges. It will be very difficult to cover up these jagged points and, indeed, they will distort any edge-stitching you try to work around the canvas.

Finish the borders of the plastic canvas with an oversewing stitch, worked from left to right, as shown in Figure 12.

Figure 12

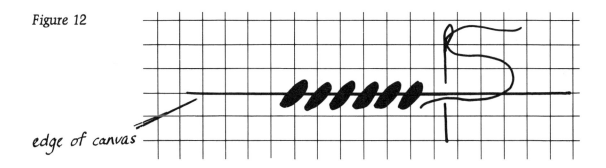

edge of canvas

Do not begin working the edge-stitching in a corner, but bring your needle up in the center of one of the sides. Work 1 stitch in each hole to the corner. Work a few extra oversewing stitches in each corner both to turn, and to cover the canvas completely. Continue working oversewing stitches until the entire border is completed.

When finishing off an end of yarn, remember to slant the yarn over the plastic and down the back of the work, as if you were in fact going to sew the next stitch (Figure 13). If you take the yarn vertically up and to the back of the canvas, you will leave an ugly gap between stitches (Figure 14).

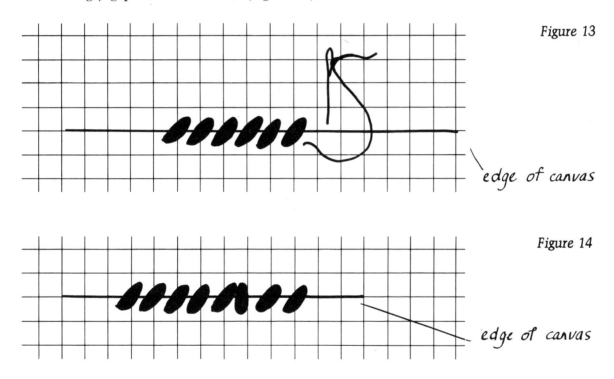

Figure 13

edge of canvas

Figure 14

edge of canvas

BLOCKING AND PRESSING

KNITTING

Knitting which is worked in Stocking Stitch, like the projects in this book, has a tendency to curl up. For pressing large items, such as afghans, you will find it convenient to use an old table, or at least one with a plastic surface which will not be spoiled by damp and warmth. A standard ironing board will not be nearly large enough for coping with an afghan. Put a blanket or some towels over the surface of the table, then an old, but clean, sheet on top. Smooth the different layers down to create a flat ironing surface. Place the section of the afghan to be pressed face down on the table thus prepared. If the edges of the afghan appear to curl round, put a few pins in to prevent this. Slant the pins so that they grip the layers of toweling or blanket below. Cut a large piece of clean, old cotton sheeting material and dampen it thoroughly in cold water. Wring out the cloth, removing all excess water.

Now place the dampened cloth over the afghan and, using a hot iron, smooth over the back of the afghan, always making sure to keep the cloth between the iron and the knitting it covers. The penetrating steam thus created will smooth out wrinkles and flatten the edges. Do not use pounding, heavy strokes, as these will leave the imprint of the iron on the work. Do not let the cloth dry out, but dampen it frequently for the maximum steaming effect.

If you own a steam iron, spraying the back of the afghan with jets of steam will produce the same effect.

While the knitting is still warm, straighten out any distortions to create a smooth finish. Carefully remove the pins, and repeat the process for each section of the afghan, until the entire surface has been "steamed" in this way. Try to leave the afghan flat, at least until the surface moisture has dried out. Hanging up damp knitting will only stretch it out of shape and defeat the purpose of pressing it.

Smaller knitted pieces may require more pinning to make them lie flat for pressing, but the basic technique remains the same as for the afghan.

CROCHET

The same procedure is followed for crochet as for knitting, except that it is rarely necessary to use any pins, since the crochet will usually lie smooth and flat from the start. Leave damp work flat to dry.

CANVAS EMBROIDERY

The same method of pressing can be used for the canvases worked in this book. There is very little distortion present with the upright stitches used. It may be necessary to repeat the steaming several times, stretching the canvas gently, while it is still damp, to make it perfectly square. Leave flat to dry.

Never apply heat to a plastic canvas. There will be no distortion at all, and therefore no need to do any pressing.

Never "press" a rug, as this will completely spoil the pile.

FRINGING CROCHET OR KNITTING

You will need a crochet hook which is not too large to go through the edge to be fringed, but large enough to firmly grip the folded yarn of the fringe itself.

With the wrong side of the work facing you, insert the crochet hook in the space to be fringed. Fold the precut lengths of yarn (four 12″ lengths for the projects in this book) in half around the top of the crochet hook. Pull this loop through to the back of the work. Catch the ends of yarn, which are now at the front of the work, in the crochet hook, and pull them through the loop on the wrong side of the work. Remove the crochet hook and pull the ends of yarn until the loop disappears, and rests snugly against the edge of the work.

MAKING A CUSHION

BOTH SIDES KNITTED AND CROCHETED

1. Place the 2 worked pieces with right sides together, and backstitch around the edge, leaving a gap wide enough for stuffing, as shown in Figure 15. Then turn right side out.

2. Insert the stuffing or pillow form through the gap.

3. Close the gap with an oversewing stitch.

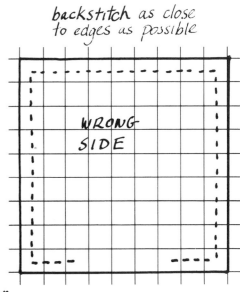

Figure 15

leave gap open

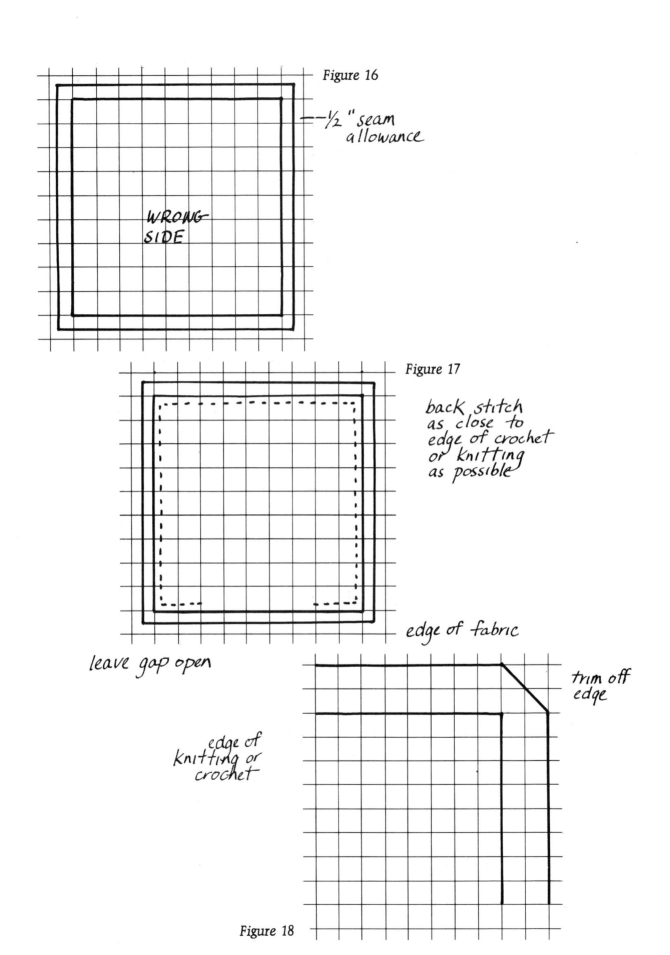

Figure 16

−½" seam
allowance

WRONG
SIDE

Figure 17

back stitch
as close to
edge of crochet
or knitting
as possible

edge of fabric

leave gap open

edge of
knitting or
crochet

trim off
edge

Figure 18

KNITTING OR CROCHET WITH A FABRIC BACKING

1. Cut the fabric ½″ larger in each direction than the knitted or crocheted side, for a seam allowance. For example, if the knitted square is 16″ × 16″, then the fabric will measure 17″ × 17″.
2. Place worked square and fabric with right sides together, with the ½″ seam allowance projecting on each side (Figure 16).
3. Backstitch around as shown in Figure 17, leaving gap wide enough for stuffing.
4. Trim the fabric at each corner as shown in Figure 18, and turn right side out.
5. Insert the stuffing or pillow form through the gap.
6. Close the gap with an oversewing stitch, turning in the ½″ seam allowance on the fabric as you sew.

GOBELIN CANVAS WITH A FABRIC BACKING

1. Trim the canvas to within ½″ of the embroidery on all sides. Now follow instructions 1 through 6 as for knitted or crocheted cushions with a fabric backing. You will have a ½″ seam allowance on the canvas as well as on the fabric, which must also be trimmed off at the corners and tucked in across the gap.

RUG CANVAS WITH A FABRIC BACKING

1. Trim the canvas, leaving 2 complete meshes as a seam allowance on each side. Follow the directions given for Gobelin canvas cushions, taking care not to catch up any of the tufts of wool as you machine sew the rug canvas to the backing fabric.

SWISS DARNING You will need a blunt-ended tapestry needle. A number 18 is a good size for the projects in this book.

1. Bring the threaded needle through from the back to the front of the work, through the center of the stitch *below* the one to be covered (Photograph 2). Leave an end of yarn at the back, which will be caught up and covered during work.

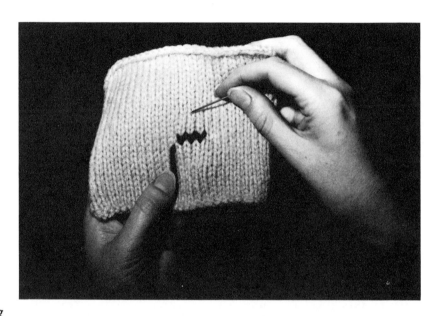

Photos 2 & 3: Swiss Darning

2. Take the needle in and out again behind the stitch in the row above (Photograph 3).

3. Finish the stitch by placing the needle into the same hole you started with, and taking it through to the back of the work. You have now covered 1 stitch of the knitting with a different color. Do not pull the yarn too tightly, but try to make the embroidered stitches blend in with the gauge of the knitting.

Cover all stitches indicated on the charts in this manner. Swiss Darning is a simple technique which gives you greater flexibility in working the knitting with more than two colors at once. Any pattern in knitting can be "applied" in this manner. Try using graph or squared paper to plot out your own motifs to brighten up a plain piece of knitting. The possibilities are only limited by the scope of your own imagination.

DESIGNING YOUR OWN PROJECTS

1. Always use graph or squared paper to plot out your design before you start work. This will avoid undesired results and unexpected problems.

2. Decide what "value" each square on your chart is going to have. For example, squares on the canvas charts in this book variously represent 6, 4, or 2 meshes of the canvas. You know how many meshes to 1″ the canvas you are working with has, and thus you will be able to determine exactly how large you want your design to be, and how many squares on the chart will represent this size. For rugs it is advisable to work with 1 square on the chart equaling 1 mesh on the canvas and 1 knot on the finished rug.

3. For knitting and crochet, you do not have a canvas with a predetermined number of meshes to the inch. Therefore you have to work out your own gauge before you start designing. Finding out how many stitches and rows you will have to the inch enables you to determine how many stitches to cast on, or chains to begin with for a foundation, to achieve the exact overall measurement you have in mind for your project. Any patterning can then be worked out on graph or squared paper before you begin.

2 . Scandinavian Designs

You will find a variety of projects to work in this chapter, all based on the motifs which occur repeatedly throughout Scandinavian decorative crafts.

The afghans are all knitted as this is a traditional Scandinavian craft. However, the same motifs are also used in canvaswork projects and rugs, so it is to be hoped that there will be something for everyone. Designs can be mixed and matched, since these folk motifs have a way of blending happily with one another. For that reason, traditional canvas-work projects appear at the end of the chapter.

Canvas squares can be sewn together to make rugs or wall hangings, or used as they are for pillows or pictures. Any of the charts provided can be used as the basis for making larger rugs with several repeats of the motif worked side by side.

The Persian Needlepoint Wool used for most of the canvas work may be changed for a 4-ply-weight yarn. This will reduce costs, and produce an exact match for the yarns used in the knitting projects. Approximate yardages are given for every item.

SCANDINAVIAN ROSE COORDINATES (Plate 1)

This delightful Scandinavian Rose motif is here translated into a knitted afghan with topstitching using the Swiss Darning technique, three Gobelin Stitch pillows, and a place mat. Should you wish to make additional coordinating items, such as a knitted cushion or a latch-hook rug, please consult Chapter 1 for general instructions on creating your own designs.

The colors red, black, and white, as used in this set are fairly commonly found in Scandinavian sweater design. However, these colors are more unusual for the home. The design retains its striking attractiveness when shades of the same color are used to work it. There should, however, be a considerable contrast in tone between the color used for the background and that used for the "petals" of the rose. Such a contrast will give the best results. A color in the range between these two can then be used for the enclosing borders.

AFGHAN IN SCANDINAVIAN ROSE PATTERN** (Photograph 4)

Finished size: Approx. 42″ × 64″ (exclusive of fringes)

You need: 4-ply acrylic or knitting worsted yarn.
5 4-oz. skeins in Black (shade A), represented on the charts by unshaded squares.
2 4-oz. skeins in Red (shade B), represented on the charts by black circles.
1 4-oz skein in White (shade C), represented on the charts by black dots
A size 10½ circular knitting needle
A size 18 tapestry needle for the Swiss Darning

Gauge: 4 sts. and 5 rows to 1″ over plain st.st. on size 10½ needle

Special Note: To make the knitting easier, where three colors occur in one row of knitting only two colors are actually knitted, the third being worked afterwards in Swiss Darning, over the appropriate stitches on the knitted background. Full instructions for working Swiss Darning are given in Chapter 1. If you are familiar with the technique of knitting with more than two colors in a row, then by all means knit the additional colors into the work. You should then follow the chart showing the completed Swiss Darning, which provides every detail of all the colors used in the design.

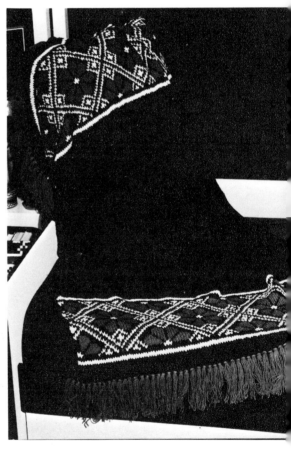

Photo 4: Afghan in Scandinavian Rose

To Make: With size 10½ circular needle and Shade A, cast on 163 sts.

IMPORTANT: The afghan is worked back and forth in the usual method for two needles. The circular needle is used only to make it easier to cope with the large number of stitches.

ROW 1: K.

ROW 2: K5, P to within last 5 sts., K5.
Repeat rows 1 and 2 until 10 rows of st.st. have been worked. Join Shade C. Begin working the chart shown in Figure 19 where indicated by the black arrow.

IMPORTANT: Keep a border of 5 sts. in K at either side of work throughout. This border of 5 sts. *is not* shown on the chart. When the chart has been completed, break off shades B and C. Continue working straight in st.st., keeping borders of K5 at

Figure 19

continue this repeat ←
across

Pattern repeat is 38 sts.

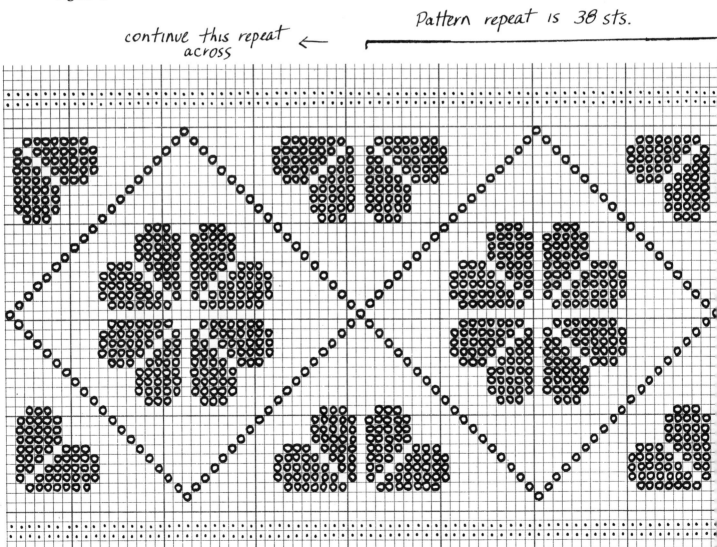

either side of work, until 166 rows have been completed in Shade A.

Work the chart shown in Figure 19 once more, break off shades B and C. Work 10 more rows in shade A. Bind off.

SWISS DARNING: Following the chart shown in Figure 20, complete the patterning in shade C on both borders.

FINISHING: Weave any loose ends along the back of the work, and give the afghan a press, following the instructions given in Chapter 1.

FRINGES: Cut four 12″ lengths of yarn in shade B for each fringe, and follow the instructions for making fringes given in Chapter 1. Space the fringes close together along upper and lower edges of the afghan, and trim the ends even, when fringing is completed.

• = Swiss Darning in white unless otherwise indicated

These two rows are knitted

Figure 20

These two rows are knitted

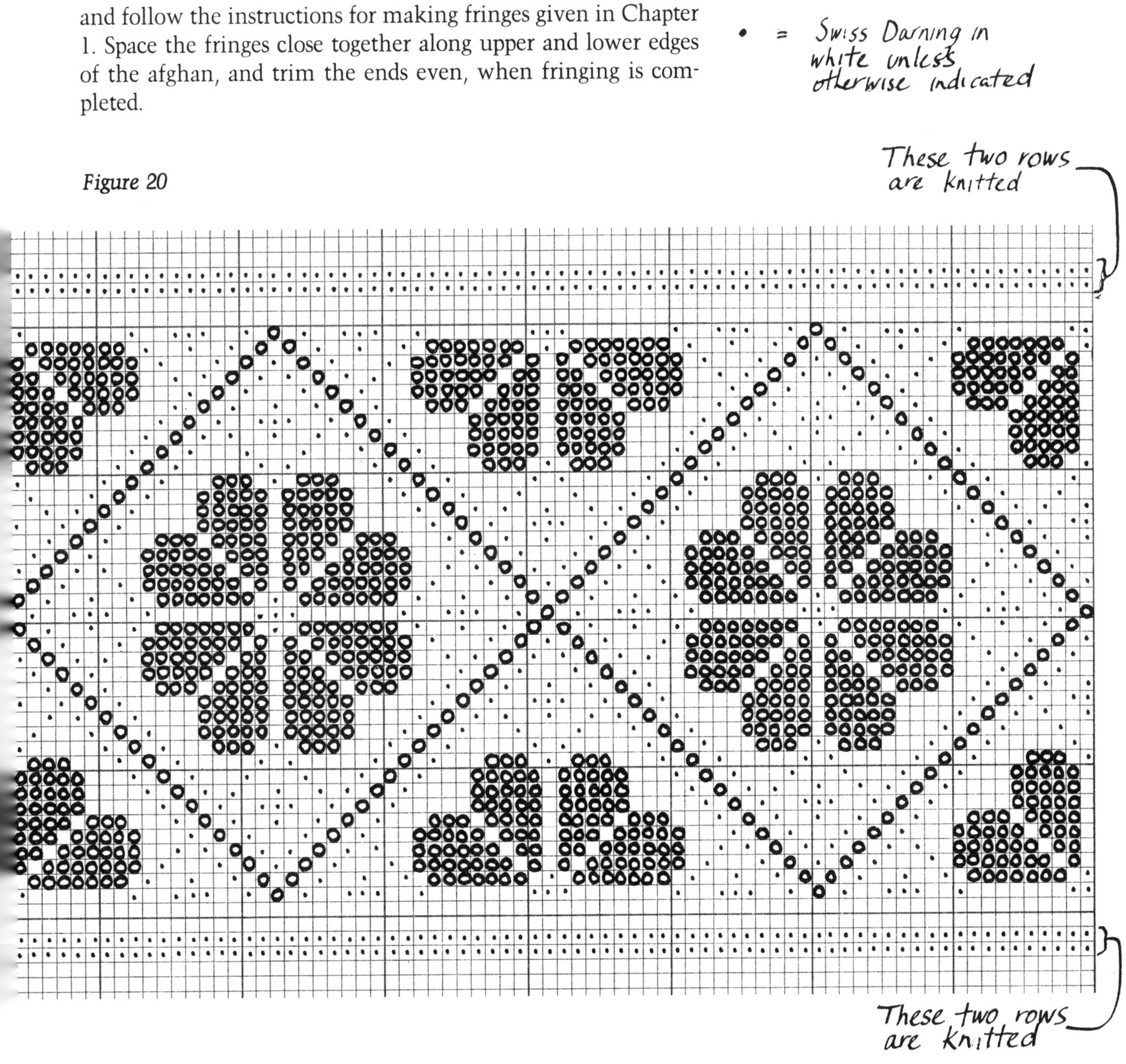

Photo 5: Pillow or Picture in Scandinavian Rose (#1)

PILLOW OR PICTURE IN SCANDINAVIAN ROSE* (Photograph 5)

Finished size: Approx. 16″ × 16″

You need: Persian Needlepoint Wool in 10-yd. skeins

Black: 10 (100 yds.)

Red: 6 (60 yds.)

White: 3 (30 yds.)

A piece of 10-mesh-to-1″ mono canvas measuring 20″ × 20″

A size 18 tapestry needle

Method:

1. The entire design is worked over 4 meshes of the canvas in Upright Gobelin Stitch.

2. Start in the lower right-hand corner, at a point 2″ up from bottom and in from side edge of canvas.

3. Following the chart in Figure 21, begin work where indicated by the arrow. Work in rows across, until entire chart is completed.

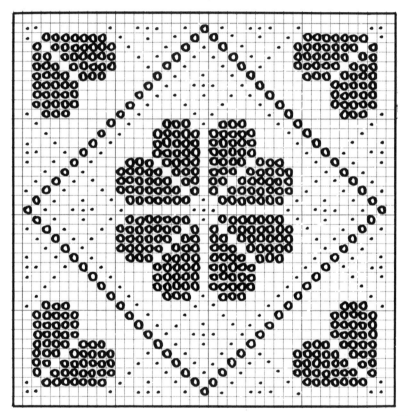

One square on chart = 4 stitches and 4 meshes on the canvas

Figure 21

Unshaded squares = Black
O = Red
· = White

PILLOW OR PICTURE IN SCANDINAVIAN ROSE** (Photograph 6)

Finished size: Approx. 16″ × 16″

You need: Persian Needlepoint Wool in 10-yd. skeins.
Black: 10 (100 yds.)
Red: 6 (60 yds.)
White: 3 (30 yds.)
A 20″ × 20″ piece of 10-mesh-to-1-inch mono canvas
A size 18 tapestry needle

Method:

1. The entire design is worked over 2 meshes of the canvas in Upright Gobelin Stitch. Advice on how to work this stitch is given in Chapter 1.

2. Start in the lower right-hand corner, at a point 2″ up from bottom and in from side edge.

3. Following the chart in Figure 22, begin work where indicated by the arrow. Work in rows across, until entire chart is completed.

Photo 6:   Pillow or Picture in Scandinavian Rose (#2)

One square on chart = 2 stitches and 2 meshes on the canvas

unshaded squares = Black
O = Red
• = White

Figure 22

RECTANGULAR PILLOW OR PICTURE IN SCANDINAVIAN ROSE*** (Photograph 7)

Finished size: Approx. 18¼″ × 11¼″

You need: Persian Needlepoint Wool in 10-yd. skeins
Black: 10 (100 yds.)
Red: 5 (50 yds.)
White: 4 (40 yds.)
A piece of 18-mesh-to-1″ mono canvas measuring 20″ × 13″
A number 22 tapestry needle

Method:

1. The entire design is worked with only 2 strands of Persian yarn instead of the usual 3. The extra strand is peeled off, starting at the center of a length and working out to the ends. The extra strands are then used in pairs as they become available.

2. The entire design is worked over 4 meshes of the canvas, using Upright Gobelin Stitch.

3. Start in lower right-hand corner, at a point 1″ up from bottom and in from side edge.

4. Following the chart shown in Figure 23, begin work where indicated by the arrow. Work in rows across, until entire chart is completed.

Photo 7:   Rectangular Pillow or Picture in Scandinavian Rose

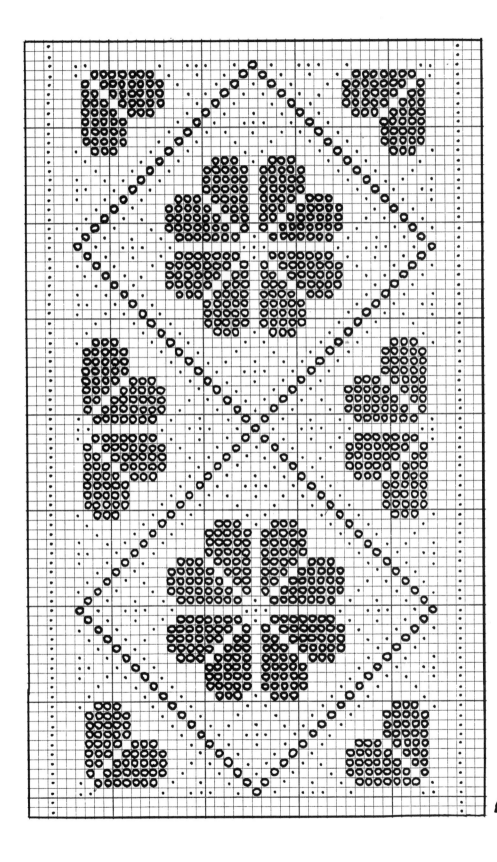

Figure 23

One square on chart = 4 stitches and 4 meshes on canvas

Unshaded squares = Black
O = Red
· = White

PLACE MAT IN SCANDINAVIAN ROSE*
(Photograph 8)

Finished size: Approx. 12½″ × 10¼″

You need: Persian Needlepoint Wool in 10-yd. skeins.
Black: 4 (40 yds.)
Red: 4 (40 yds.)
White: 4 (40 yds.)
A rectangular piece of plastic canvas with 7 holes to 1″, measuring 13¼″ × 10½″
A number 18 tapestry needle

Method:

1. The entire design is worked in blocks of the diagonal stitch shown in Chapter 1.

2. One square on the chart shown in Figure 24 is equivalent to 1 completed block of diagonal stitches.

3. Start in the lower right-hand corner, making sure that you work right up to the edge of the canvas (Figure 11). This will reduce the amount of trimming required at the end of work.

4. Following the chart in Figure 24, begin work where indicated by the arrow. Work in rows of blocks across, until entire chart is completed.

5. Trim away excess plastic as shown in Photograph 1.

6. Choose 1 of the colors in the design for the stitched edging. Work in an oversewing stitch from left to right as shown in Figure 12, and described in Chapter 1.

7. *Do not press.*

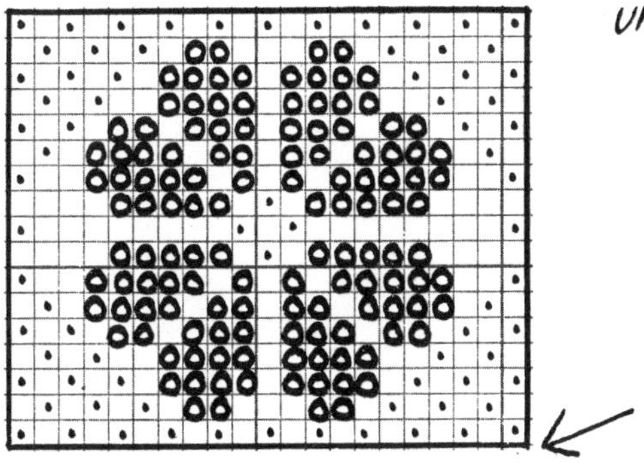

One square on
canvas = one
block of
stitches

unshaded squares = Black
O = Red
• = White

Figure 24

Photo 8:   *Place Mat in
Scandinavian Rose*

WINDBLOWN SNOWFLAKES COORDINATES (Plate 2)

The half-snowflake motif used in the following group of designs appears to move at the speed of blizzard-force gusts. I have accentuated this feeling by choosing cold colors, the shades of blue with white which one associates with snow and ice. You can decide on your own color schemes to suit your particular decorating needs.

The group of designs includes instructions for a knitted afghan and cushion, two pillow or picture squares worked in Upright Gobelin Stitch, a decorative strip for a cushion, and a place mat. Should you wish to make additional items, such as a latch-hook rug, please consult Chapter 1 for general instructions on how to create your own designs.

AFGHAN IN WINDBLOWN SNOWFLAKES**
(Photograph 9)

Finished size: Approx. 46" × 75" (exclusive of fringes)

You need: 4-ply acrylic or knitting worsted yarn
7   4-oz skeins in Medium Blue (shade A), represented on the charts by unshaded squares
2   4-oz. skeins in White (shade B), represented on the charts by black circles
1   4 oz. skein in Royal Blue (shade C), represented on the charts by black dots
1   4-oz. skein in Navy Blue (shade D), represented on the charts by black crosses
A size 10½ circular knitting needle
A number 18 tapestry needle for the Swiss Darning

Gauge: 4 sts. and 5 rows to 1" over plain st.st. on size 10½ needle

Special Note: To make the knitting easier where three colors occur in 1 row of knitting, only two colors are actually knitted, the third being worked afterwards, in Swiss Darning, over the appropriate stitches on the knitted background. Full instructions for working Swiss Darning are given in Chapter 1. If you are familiar with the technique of knitting with more than two colors in a row, then by all means knit the additional colors into the work. You should then follow the chart showing the completed Swiss Darning, which provides every detail of all the colors used in the design.

Photo 9: Afghan in Windblown Snowflakes

To Make: With size 10½ circular needle and shade A, cast on 163 sts.

IMPORTANT: The afghan is worked back and forth in the usual method for two needles. The circular needle is used only to make it easier to cope with the large number of stitches.

ROW 1: K.

ROW 2: K4, P to within last 4 sts., K4.

Repeat Rows 1 and 2 until 10 rows of st.st. have been worked. Join shade C. Begin working the chart shown in Figure 25 where indicated by the black arrow. Work 7 bands of the 37-row pattern. Repeat the border pattern once more.

IMPORTANT: Keep a border of 4 sts. in K at either side of work throughout. This border of 4 sts. *is not* shown on the chart. Finish with 10 rows in st.st. in shade A. Bind off.

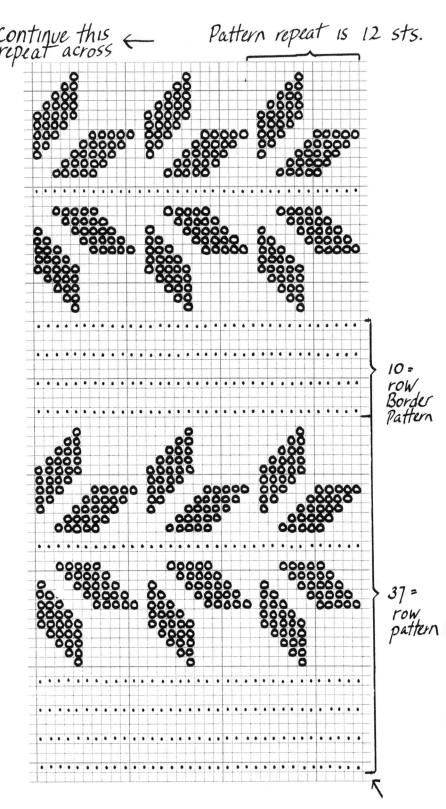

Figure 25

SWISS DARNING: Following the chart shown in Figure 26, complete the patterning in shade D in each band.

FINISHING: Weave any loose ends along the back of the work, and give the afghan a press, following the instructions given in Chapter 1.

FRINGES: Cut four 12″ lengths of yarn in shade D for each fringe, and follow the instructions given in Chapter 1 for making fringes. Space the fringes close together along upper and lower edges of the afghan, and trim the ends even, when fringing is completed.

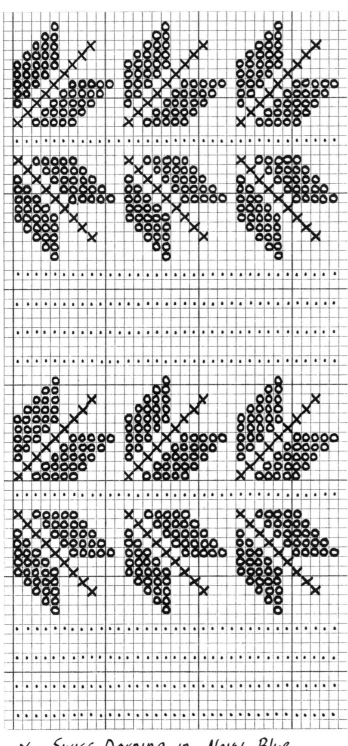

X = Swiss Darning in Navy Blue

Figure 26

KNITTED CUSHION SQUARE IN WINDBLOWN SNOWFLAKES** (Plate 2)

Finished size: Approx. 16″ × 16″

Please note: You may well have sufficient yarn left over from the afghan to make the cushion cover. However, if you want to make it as a separate item, yarn amounts are given below. You will have enough yarn to make both sides of the cushion knitted, or you may prefer to back the knitting with a fabric in a matching or toning color.

You need: 4-ply acrylic or knitting worsted yarn
1 4-oz. skein in Medium Blue (shade A) represented on the charts by unshaded squares
1 4-oz. skein in White (shade B), represented on the charts by black circles
1 4-oz. skein in Royal Blue (shade C), represented on the charts by black dots
A few sewing lengths of Navy Blue (shade D), represented on the charts by black crosses
A pair of size 7 needles
A number 18 tapestry needle for the Swiss Darning

Gauge: 4½ sts. and 6 rows to 1″ over plain st.st. on size 7 needles

Special Note: To make the knitting easier where three colors occur in 1 row of knitting, only two colors are actually knitted, the third being worked afterwards in Swiss Darning, over the appropriate stitches on the knitted background. Full instructions for working Swiss Darning are given in Chapter 1. If you are familiar with the technique of knitting with more than two colors in a row, then by all means knit the additional colors into the work. You should then follow the chart showing the completed Swiss Darning, which provides every detail of all the colors used in the design.

To Make: With size 7 needles and shade A, cast on 73 sts. Work 4 rows in st.st. Join shade C. Begin working the chart shown in Figure 27 where indicated by the black arrow. Finish with 4 rows in st.st. in shade A. Bind off.

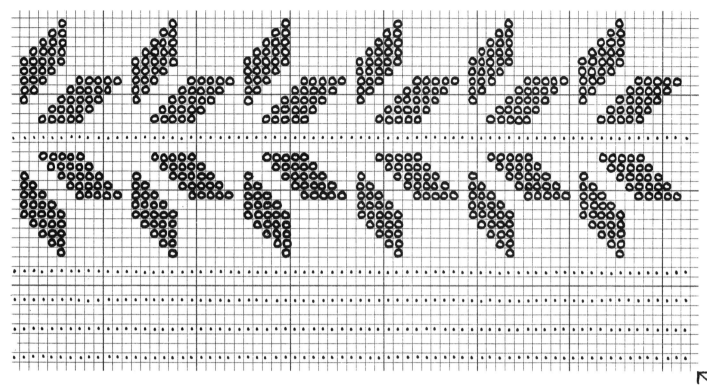

Figure 27

37-row pattern is repeated twice

finish with 12-row border pattern (3rd repeat)

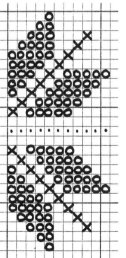

X = Swiss Darning in Navy Blue

Finish each half-snowflake motif in this way

SWISS DARNING: Following the chart shown in Figure 28, complete the patterning in shade D in each band.

FINISHING: Weave any loose ends along the back of the work, and give the cushion square a press, following the instructions given in Chapter 1. Instructions for making squares into cushions will also be found in the same chapter.

Figure 28

PILLOW OR PICTURE IN WINDBLOWN SNOWFLAKES* (Photograph 10)

Finished size: Approx. 14″ × 14″

You need: Persian Needlepoint Wool in 10-yd. skeins
White: 8 (80 yds.)
Royal Blue: 4 (40 yds.)
Navy Blue: 4 (40 yds.)
Medium Blue: 2 (20 yds.)
A piece of 10-mesh-to-1″ mono canvas measuring 18″ × 18″
A number 18 tapestry needle

Method:

1. The entire design is worked over 4 meshes of the canvas in Upright Gobelin Stitch.

2. Start in the lower right-hand corner, at a point 2″ up from bottom and in from side edge.

3. Following the chart in Figure 29, begin work where indicated by the arrow. Work in rows across, until entire chart is completed.

Photo 10:   Pillow or Picture in Windblown Snowflakes (#1)

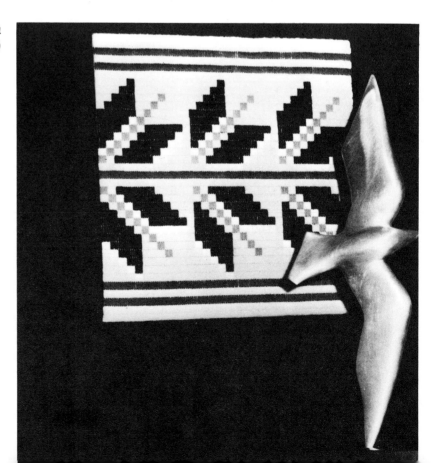

One square on chart = 4 stitches and 4 meshes on the canvas

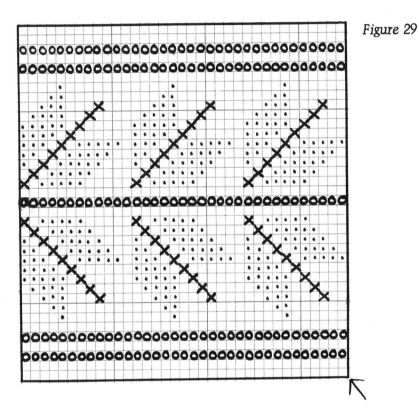

Figure 29

unshaded square = White
o = Royal Blue
· = Navy
x = Medium Blue

PILLOW OR PICTURE IN WINDBLOWN SNOWFLAKES** (Photograph 11)

Finished size: Approx. 14″ × 14″

You need: Persian Needlepoint Wool in 10-yd. skeins
White: 11 (110 yds.)
Navy: 9 (90 yds.)
Medium Blue: 1 (10 yds.)
Royal Blue: 3 (30 yds.)
A piece of 10-mesh-to-1″ mono canvas measuring 18″ × 18″
A number 18 tapestry needle

Method:

1. The entire design is worked over 2 meshes of the canvas in Upright Gobelin Stitch. Advice on how to work this stitch is given in Chapter 1.

2. Start in the lower right-hand corner, at a point 2″ up from bottom and in from side edge.

3. Following the chart in Figure 30, begin work where indicated by the arrow. Work in rows across, until entire chart is completed.

Photo 11: Pillow or Picture in Windblown Snowflakes (#2)

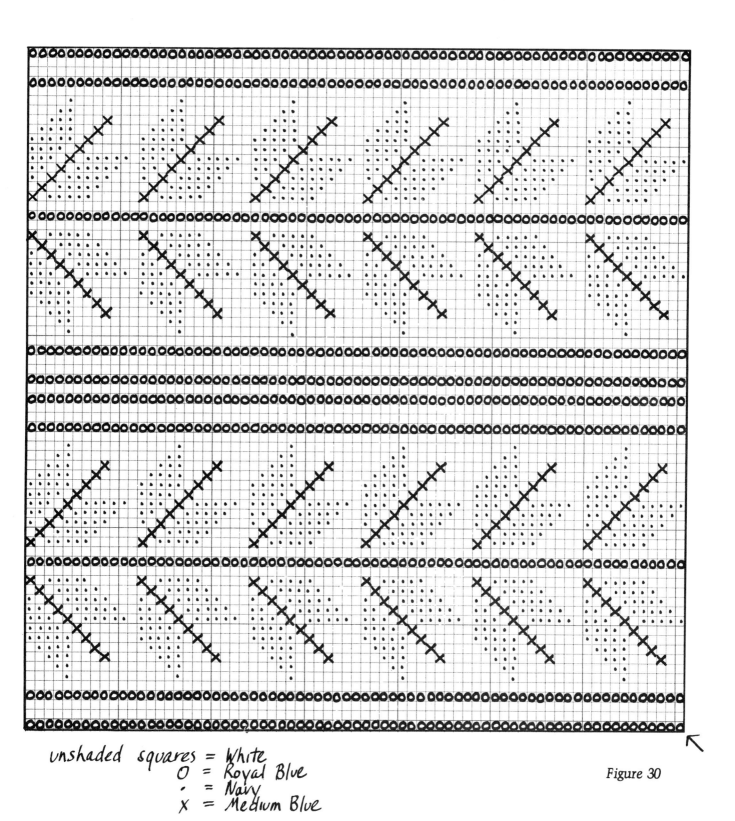

unshaded squares = White
O = Royal Blue
. = Navy
x = Medium Blue

Figure 30

One square on chart = 2 stitches and 2 holes on the canvas

CUSHION STRIP IN WINDBLOWN SNOWFLAKES** (Photograph 12)

Finished size: Approx. 16″ × 3″

You need: Persian Needlepoint Wool in 10-yd. skeins
White: 3 (30 yds.)
Navy: 2 (20 yds.)
Medium Blue: 1 (10 yds.)
Royal Blue: 1 (10 yds.)
A piece of 18-mesh-to-1″ mono canvas measuring 18″ × 5″
A number 22 tapestry needle

Special Note: Strips of Gobelin Embroidery can be decoratively applied to plain fabric pillows.

Method:

1. The entire design is worked with only 2 strands of Persian yarn instead of the usual 3. The extra strand is peeled off, starting at the center of a length and working out to the ends. The extra strands are then used in pairs as they become available.

2. The entire design is worked over 4 meshes of the canvas, using Upright Gobelin Stitch.

3. Start in lower right-hand corner, at a point 1″ up from bottom and in from side edge.

4. Following the chart shown in Figure 31, begin work where indicated by the arrow. Work in rows across, until entire chart is completed.

Figure 31

One square on chart = 4 stitches and 4 meshes on canvas

unshaded squares = White
O = Royal Blue
. = Navy
X = Medium Blue

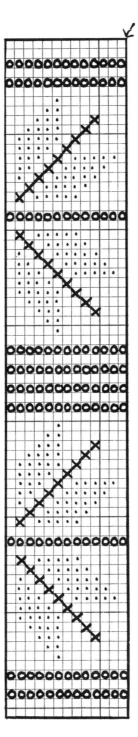

Photo 12: Cushion Strip in Windblown Snowflakes

PLACE MAT IN WINDBLOWN SNOWFLAKES*
(Photograph 13)

Finished size: Approx. 12½″ × 9½″

You need: Persian Needlepoint Wool in 10-yd. skeins
White: 5 (50 yds.)
Navy: 3 (30 yds.)
Medium Blue: 1 (10 yds.)
Royal Blue: 2 (20 yds.)
A rectangular piece of plastic canvas with 7 holes to 1″, measuring 13¼″ × 10½″
A number 18 tapestry needle

Method:

1. The entire design is worked in blocks of the Diagonal Stitch shown in Chapter 1.

2. One square on the chart shown in Figure 32 is equivalent to 1 completed block of diagonal stitches.

3. Start in the lower right-hand corner, making sure that you work right up to the edge of the canvas (Figure 11). This will reduce the amount of trimming required at the end of work.

4. Following the chart in Figure 32, begin work where indicated by the arrow. Work in rows of blocks across, until entire chart is completed.

5. Trim away excess plastic as shown in Photograph 1.

6. Choose 1 of the colors in the design for the stitched edging. Work in an oversewing stitch from left to right as shown in Figure 12, and described in Chapter 1.

7. *Do not press.*

Photo 13:   Place Mat in
Windblown Snowflakes

One square on chart = one block of stitches

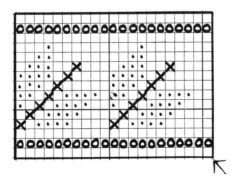

Unshaded squares = White
        o = Royal Blue
        · = Navy
        x = Medium Blue

Figure 32

ENCLOSED FLOWERS COORDINATES (Plate 3)

This simple, but effective, flower motif enclosed in diamonds was taken from a Scandinavian knitting pattern. Red flowers are worked on a snowy-white ground, and encased in a trelliswork picked out in black.

This group of designs includes instructions for a knitted afghan and cushion, two pillow or picture squares worked in Upright Gobelin Stitch, a decorative cushion strip, and a place mat worked on plastic canvas. Should you wish to make additional items, such as a latch-hook rug, please consult Chapter 1 for general instructions on how to create your own designs.

AFGHAN IN ENCLOSED FLOWERS**
(Photograph 14)

Finished size: Approx. 46" × 70" (exclusive of fringes)

You need: 4-ply acrylic or knitting worsted yarn
7 4-oz. skeins in White (shade A), represented on the charts by the unshaded squares
3 4-oz. skeins in Black (shade B), represented on the charts by black circles
2 4-oz. skeins in Red (shade C), represented on the charts by black dots
A size 10½ circular knitting needle
A number 18 tapestry needle for the Swiss Darning

Gauge: 4 sts. and 5 rows to 1" over plain st.st. on size 10½ needles

Special Note: To make the knitting easier, where three colors occur in 1 row of knitting, only two colors are actually knitted, the third being worked afterwards, in Swiss Darning over the appropriate stitches on the knitted background. Full instructions for working Swiss Darning are given in Chapter 1. If you are familiar with the technique of knitting with more than two colors in a row, then by all means knit the additional colors into the work. You should then follow the chart showing the completed Swiss Darning, which provides every detail of all the colors used in the design.

Photo 14: Afghan in Enclosed Flowers

To Make: With size 10½ circular needle and shade A, cast on 163 sts.

IMPORTANT: The afghan is worked back and forth in the usual method for two needles. The circular needle is used only to make it easier to cope with the large number of stitches.

ROW 1: K.

ROW 2: K3, P to within last 3 sts., K3.
Repeat rows 1 and 2 until 10 rows of st.st. have been worked.
Join shade B and repeat rows 1 and 2 once more.
Change to shade A and repeat rows 1 and 2.
Begin working the chart shown in Figure 33 where indicated by the black arrow. The 12-row pattern repeat is repeated 20 times in all. Work first row of pattern once more to complete last row of diamonds.

IMPORTANT: Keep a border of 3 sts. in K at either side of work throughout. This border of 3 sts. *is not* shown on the chart. Finish with rows 1 and 2 in shade A, then in shade B, and then 10 rows of plain st.st. in shade A. Bind off.

SWISS DARNING: Following the chart shown in Figure 34, complete the patterning in shade C in each diamond.

FINISHING: Weave any loose ends along the back of the work, and give the afghan a press, following the instructions given in Chapter 1.

FRINGES: Cut four 12″ lengths of yarn in shade B for each fringe, and follow the instructions given in Chapter 1 for making fringes. Space the fringes close together along upper and lower edges of the afghan, and trim the ends even, when fringing is completed.

continue this repeat
across ←

pattern repeat is
12 sts.

Figure 33

12-row pattern

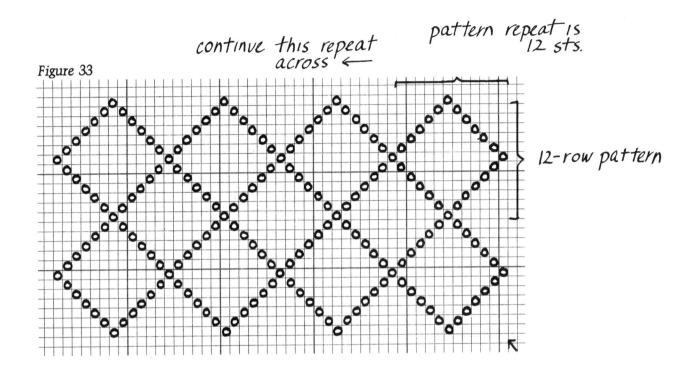

Figure 34

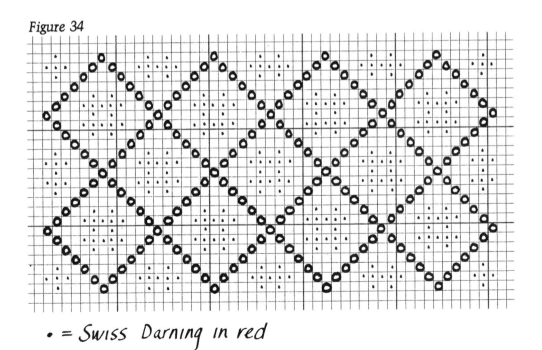

• = Swiss Darning in red

KNITTED CUSHION SQUARE IN ENCLOSED FLOWERS** (Figure 35)

Finished size: Approx. 16″ × 16″

Please note: You may well have sufficient yarn left over from the afghan to make the cushion cover. However, if you want to make it as a separate item, your amounts are given below. You will have enough yarn to make both sides of the cushion knitted, or you may prefer to back the knitting with a fabric in a matching or toning color.

You need:
4-ply acrylic or knitting worsted yarn
1 4-oz. skein in White (shade A), represented in the charts by unshaded squares
1 4-oz. skein in Black (shade B), represented on the charts by black circles
1 4-oz. skein in Red (shade C), represented on the charts by black dots
A pair of size 7 needles
A number 18 tapestry needle for the Swiss Darning

Gauge: 4½ sts. and 6 rows to 1″ over plain st.st. on size 7 needles

Special Note: To make the knitting easier, where three colors occur in 1 row of knitting, only two colors are actually knitted, the third being worked afterwards, in Swiss Darning, over the appropriate stitches on the knitted background. Full instructions for working Swiss Darning are given in Chapter 1. If you are familiar with the technique of knitting with more than two colors in a row, then by all means knit the additional colors into the work. You should then follow the chart showing the completed Swiss Darning, which provides every detail of all the colors used in the design.

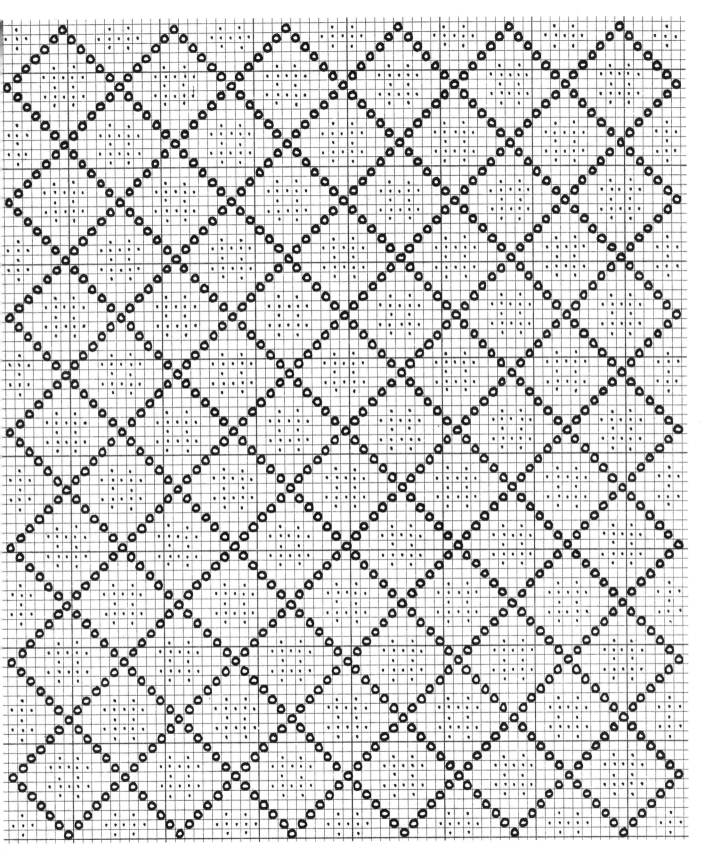

• = Swiss Darning in red

Figure 35

To make: With size 7 needles and shade A, cast on 73 sts. Work 2 rows in st.st. Join shade B.
Begin working the chart shown in Figure 36, where indicated by the black arrow.
Work 2 rows in st.st. in shade A. Bind off.

SWISS DARNING: Following the chart shown in Figure 35, complete the patterning in shade C in each diamond.

FINISHING: Weave all the loose ends along the back of the work, and give the cushion square a press, following the instructions given in Chapter 1. Instructions for making squares into cushions will also be found in the same chapter.

Figure 36

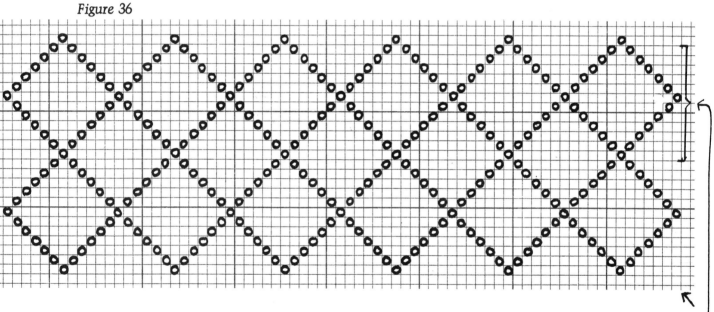

12-row pattern is repeated 7 times

PILLOW OR PICTURE IN ENCLOSED FLOWERS*
(Photograph 15)

Finished size: Approx. 16″ × 16″

You need: Persian Needlepoint Wool in 10-yd.
skeins
White: 10 (100 yds.)
Black: 3 (30 yds.)
Red: 3 (30 yds.)
A piece of 10-mesh-to-1″ mono canvas
measuring 20″ × 20″
A number 18 tapestry needle

*Photo 15: Pillow or Picture in
Enclosed Flowers #1*

Method:

1. The entire design is worked over 4 meshes of the canvas in Upright Gobelin Stitch.

2. Start in the lower right-hand corner, at a point 2″ up from bottom and in from side edge.

3. Following the chart in Figure 37, begin work where indicated by the arrow. Work in rows across, until entire chart is completed.

Figure 37

One square on chart =
 4 stitches and 4 meshes
 on canvas

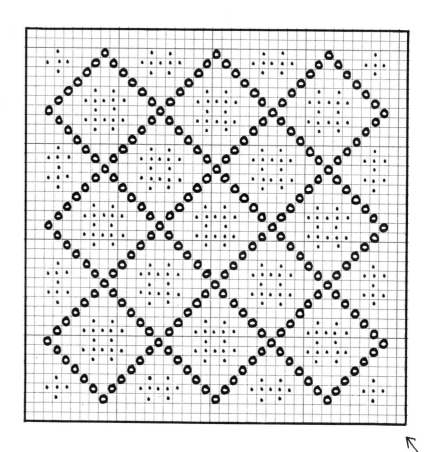

Unshaded squares = White
 0 = Black
 · = Red

CUSHION STRIP IN ENCLOSED FLOWERS***
(Photograph 16)

Finished size: Approx. 16½″ × 3″

You need: Persian Needlepoint Wool in 10-yd. skeins
White: 3 (30 yds.)
Black: 2 (20 yds.)
Red: 2 (20 yds.)
A piece of 18-mesh-to-1″ mono canvas measuring 19″ × 5″
A number 22 tapestry needle

Special Note: Strips of Gobelin Embroidery can be decoratively applied to plain fabric pillows.

Method:

1. The entire design is worked with only 2 strands of Persian yarn instead of the usual 3. The extra strand is peeled off, starting at the center of a length and working out to the ends. The extra strands are then used in pairs as they become available.

2. The entire design is worked over 4 meshes of the canvas, using Upright Gobelin Stitch.

3. Start in lower right-hand corner, at a point 1″ up from bottom and in from side edge.

4. Following the chart shown in Figure 38, begin work where indicated by the arrow. Work in rows across, until entire chart is completed.

Photo 16: Cushion Strip in Enclosed Flowers

Figure 38

One square on chart = 4 stitches and 4 meshes on canvas

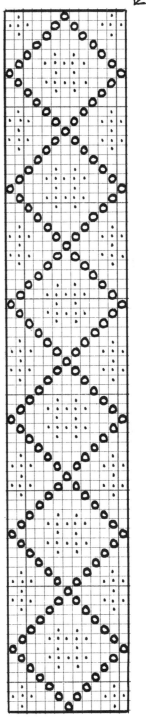

Unshaded squares = White
0 = Black
• = Red

PILLOW OR PICTURE IN ENCLOSED FLOWERS**
(Plate 3)

Finished size: Approx. 14″ × 14″

You need: Persian Needlepoint Wool in 10 yd.
skeins
White: 9 (90 yds.)
Black: 3 (30 yds.)
Red: 3 (30 yds.)
A piece of 10-mesh-to-1″ mono canvas
measuring 18″ × 18″
A number 18 tapestry needle

Method:

1. The entire design is worked over 2 meshes of the canvas in Upright Gobelin Stitch. Advice on how to work this stitch is given in Chapter 1.

2. Start in the lower right-hand corner, at a point 2″ up from bottom and in from side edge.

3. Following the chart in Figure 39, begin work where indicated by the arrow. Work in rows across, until entire chart is completed.

One square on chart = 2 stitches and 2 meshes on canvas

Figure 39

unshaded squares = White
O = Black
. = Red

PLACE MAT IN ENCLOSED FLOWERS*
(Photograph 17)

Finished size: Approx. 12½″ × 10¼″

You need: Persian Needlepoint Wool in 10-yd. skeins.
White: 4 (40 yds.)
Black: 2 (20 yds.)
Red: 3 (30 yds.)
A rectangular piece of plastic canvas, with 7 holes to 1″, measuring 13¼ ″ × 10½″
A number 18 tapestry needle

Method:

1. The entire design is worked in blocks of the Diagonal Stitch shown in Chapter 1.

2. One square on the chart shown in Figure 40 is equivalent to 1 completed block of diagonal stitches.

3. Start in the lower right-hand corner, making sure that you work right up to the edge of the canvas (Figure 11). This will reduce the amount of trimming required at the end of work.

4. Following the chart in Figure 40, begin work where indicated by the arrow. Work in rows of blocks across, until entire chart is completed.

5. Trim away excess plastic as shown in Photograph 1.

6. Choose 1 of the colors in the design for the stitched edging. Work in an oversewing stitch from left to right as shown in Figure 12 and described in Chapter 1.

7. *Do not press.*

Photo 17: Place Mat in
Enclosed Flowers

Figure 40

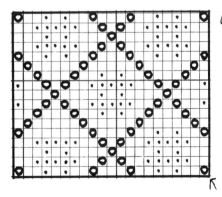

unshaded squares = White
o = Black
• = Red

One square on chart = one block of stitches

FLEUR-DE-LYS COORDINATES (Plate 4)

This Scandinavian version of the Fleur-de-Lys motif is used here in the design for a knitted afghan, and two pillows or pictures in Upright Gobelin Stitch. The motif could very suitably be used for a rug design. Instructions for how to create your own designs can be found in Chapter 1.

FLEUR-DE-LYS AFGHAN* (Photograph 18)

Finished size: Approx. 44″ × 65″ (exclusive of fringes)

You need: 4-ply acrylic or knitting worsted yarn
5 4-oz. skeins in Kelly Green (shade A), represented on the chart by unshaded squares
2 4-oz. skeins in Turquoise (shade B), represented on the chart by black circles
2 4-oz. skeins in Royal Blue (shade C), represented on the chart by black dots
A size 10½ circular knitting needle

Gauge: 4 sts. and 5 rows to 1″ over plain st.st. on size 10½ needles

To make: With size 10½ circular needle and shade A, cast on 163 sts.

IMPORTANT: The afghan is worked back and forth in the usual method for two needles. The circular needle is used only to make it easier to cope with the large number of stitches.

ROW 1: K.

ROW 2: K3, P to within last 3 sts, K3.
Repeat Rows 1 and 2 until 8 rows of st.st. have been worked in Shade A, join shade B.
Begin working the chart shown in Figure 41 where indicated by the black arrow.
Continue alternating bands 1 and 2, always working 16 rows in shade A between each band, until Band 1 has been worked for the fourth time.

IMPORTANT Keep a border of 3 sts. in K at either side of work throughout. This border of 3 sts *is not* shown on the chart. Work 8 rows in st.st. in shade A. Bind off.

Photo 18:   Fleur-de-Lys Afghan

FINISHING: Weave any loose ends along the back of the work, and give the afghan a press, following the instructions given in Chapter 1.

FRINGES: Cut four 12″ lengths of yarn for each fringe. Alternate shade A and C for the fringes and follow the instructions given in Chapter 1 for applying the fringes to the afghan. Space the fringes fairly close together along upper and lower edges of the afghan, and trim the ends even, when fringing is completed.

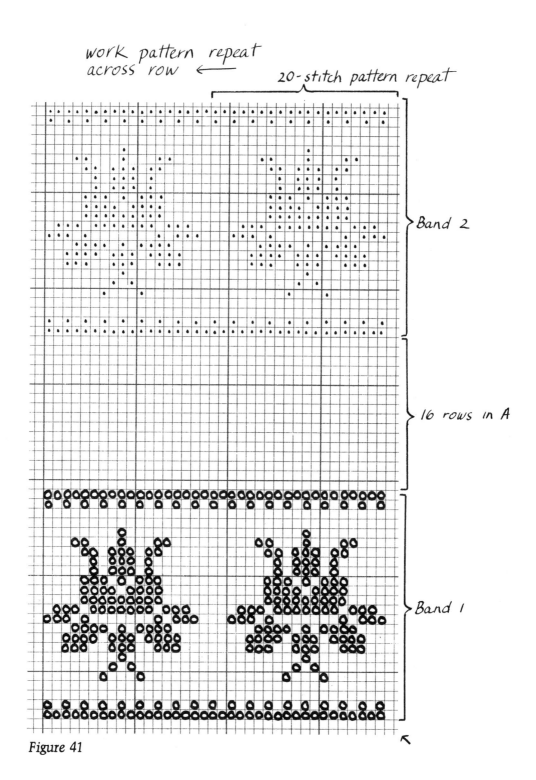

work pattern repeat
across row ←

20-stitch pattern repeat

Band 2

16 rows in A

Band 1

Figure 41

FLEUR-DE-LYS PILLOW OR PICTURE** (Plate 4)

Finished size: Approx. 16″ × 16″

You need: Persian Needlepoint Wool in 10-yd. skeins.
Kelly Green: 8 (80 yds.)
Royal Blue: 6 (60 yds.)
A piece of 10-mesh-to-1″ mono canvas measuring 20″ × 20″
A number 18 tapestry needle

Method:

1. The entire design is worked over 4 meshes of the canvas in Upright Gobelin Stitch.

2. Start in the lower right-hand corner, at a point 2″ up from bottom and in from side edge.

3. Following the chart in Figure 42, begin work where indicated by the arrow. Work in rows across, until entire chart is completed.

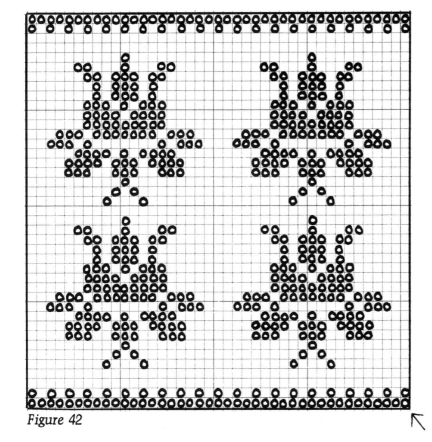

Figure 42

One square on chart = 4 stitches and 4 meshes on canvas

Unshaded squares = Kelly Green

ⵔ = Royal Blue

FLEUR-DE-LYS PILLOW OR PICTURE**
(Photograph 19)

Finished size: Approx. 16″ × 16″

You need: Persian Needlepoint Wool in 10-yd.
skeins
Royal Blue: 13 (130 yds.)
Turquoise: 3 (30 yds.)
Kelly Green: 3 (30 yds.)
A piece of 10-mesh-to-1″ mono canvas
measuring 20″ × 20″
A number 18 tapestry needle

Method:

1. The entire design is worked over 2 meshes of the canvas
in Upright Gobelin Stitch. Advice on how to work this
stitch is given in Chapter 1.

2. Start in the lower right-hand corner, at a point 2″ up
from bottom and in from side edge.

3. Following the chart in Figure 43, begin work where indicated by the arrow. Work in rows across, until entire
chart is completed.

Photo 19:   *Fleur-de-Lys Pillow
or Picture (#2)*

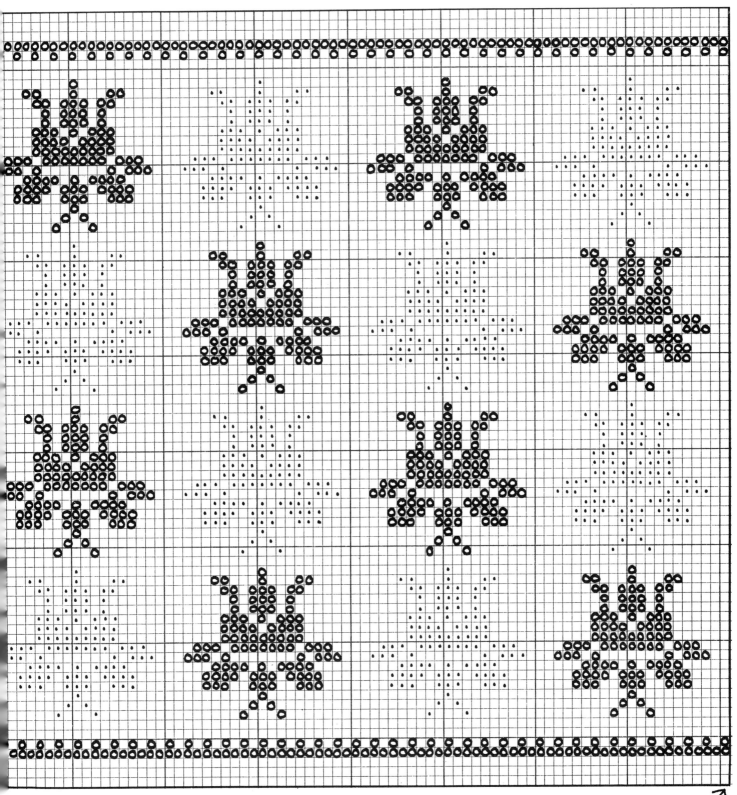

Figure 43

One square on chart = 2 stitches and 2 meshes on canvas
Unshaded squares = Royal Blue
      0 = Turquoise
      · = Kelly Green

HEART MOTIF COORDINATES (Plate 5)

The heart motif occurs in many folk traditions, and has always proved a popular way of putting a little more love into handwork. The designs which follow are mostly worked in red and white. Occasionally, to vary the theme a little, I have worked red hearts on a black background. There is no reason why you should not try entirely different colors for your own projects.

You can make your selection from among a wide variety of items: a knitted afghan and cushion; two pillows or cushion squares worked in Upright Gobelin Stitch; a square pillow worked in rug wool using a latch hook; a decorative cushion strip in Upright Gobelin Stitch, and two place mat designs to work on plastic canvas.

HEART MOTIF AFGHAN* (Photograph 20)

Finished size: Approx. 47" × 60" (Exclusive of fringes)

You need: 4-ply acrylic or knitting worsted yarn
5 4-oz. skeins in White (shade A), represented on the chart by unshaded squares
4 4-oz. skeins in Red (shade B), represented on the chart by black circles.
A size 10½ circular needle

Gauge: 4 sts. and 5 rows to 1" over plain st.st. on size 10½ needles.

To Make: With size 10½ circular needle and shade A, cast on 167 sts.

IMPORTANT: The afghan is worked back and forth in the usual method for two needles. The circular needle is used only to make it easier to cope with the large number of stitches.

ROW 1: K

ROW 2: K3, P to within last 3 sts., K3.
Repeat rows 1 and 2 until 24 rows in st.st. have been worked in shade A, join shade B.
Begin working the chart shown in Figure 44 where indicated by the black arrow.

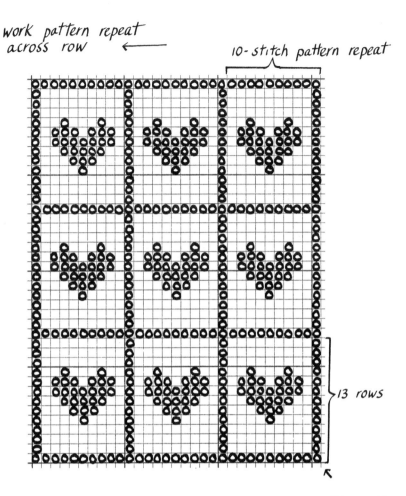

Figure 44

Work 18 repeats of the 13-row pattern, and Row 1 of the pattern once more to complete the last boxes.

IMPORTANT: Keep a border of 3 sts. in K at either side of work throughout. This border of 3 sts. *is not* shown on the chart. Finish with 24 rows in st.st. in shade A. Bind off.

FINISHING: Weave any loose ends along the back of the work, and give the afghan a press, following the instructions given in Chapter 1.

FRINGES: Cut four 12″ lengths of yarn in shade B, for each fringe, and follow the instructions given in Chapter 1 for making fringes. Space the fringes close together along upper and lower edges of the afghan, and trim the ends even, when fringing is completed.

KNITTED CUSHION SQUARE IN HEART MOTIF* (Photograph 20)

Finished size: Approx. 16″ × 16″

Please note: You may well have sufficient yarn left over from the afghan to make the cushion cover. However, if you want to make it as a separate item, your amounts are given below. You will have enough yarn to make both sides of the cushion knitted, or you may prefer to back the knitting with a fabric in a matching or toning color.

You need: 4-ply acrylic or knitting worsted yarn
1 4-oz. skein in White (shade A), represented on the chart by unshaded squares
1 4-oz. skein in Red (shade B), represented on the chart by black circles
A pair of size 7 needles

Gauge: 4½ sts. and 6 rows to 1″ over plain st.st. on size 7 needles

To Make: With size 7 needles and shade B, cast on 71 sts. Begin working the chart shown in Figure 45 where indicated by the black arrow.

When chart has been completed, bind off in shade B.

Finishing: Weave all the loose ends along the back of the work, and give the cushion square a press, following the instructions given in Chapter 1. Instructions for making squares into cushions will also be found in the same chapter.

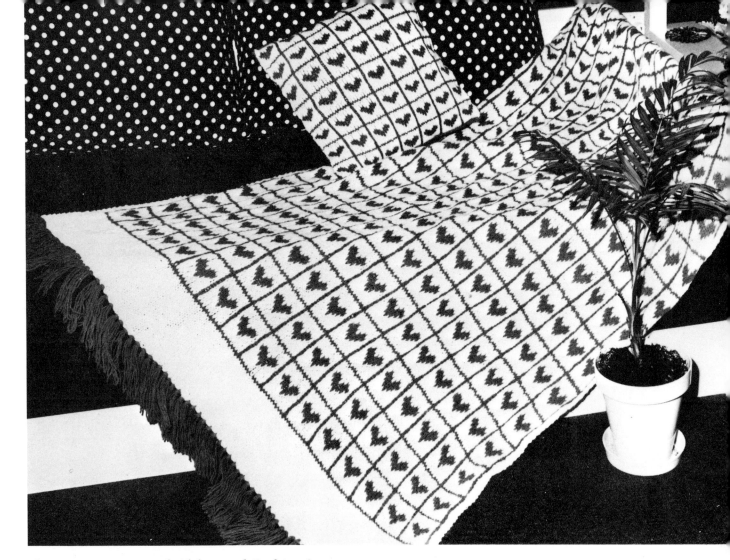

Photo 20:   Heart Motif Afghan and Cushion Square

Figure 45

13-row
pattern is
repeated
until
7 rows of
hearts are
completed

HEART MOTIF PILLOW OR PICTURE*
(Photograph 21)

Finished size: Approx. 16″ × 16″

You need: Persian Needlepoint Wool in 10-yd. skeins
Black: 12 (120 yds.)
Red: 8 (80 yds.)
A piece of 10-mesh-to-1″ mono canvas measuring 20″ × 20″
A number 18 tapestry needle

Photo 21:   Heart Motif Pillow or Picture (#1)

Method:

1. The entire design is worked over 4 meshes of the canvas in Upright Gobelin Stitch.

2. Start in the lower right-hand corner, at a point 2″ up from bottom and in from side edge.

3. Following the chart in Figure 46, begin work where indicated by the arrow. Work in rows across, until entire chart is completed.

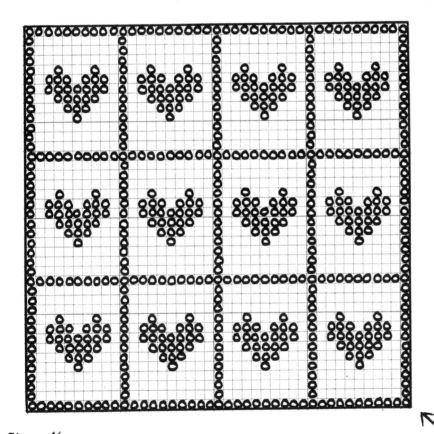

One square on chart =
4 stitches and 4
meshes on canvas

Unshaded squares = Black
0 = Red

Figure 46

HEART MOTIF PILLOW OR PICTURE**
(Photograph 22)

Finished size: Approx. 14″ × 14″

You need: Persian Needlepoint Wool in 10-yd. skeins
White: 9 (90 yds.)
Red: 6 (60 yds.)
A piece of 10-mesh-to-1″ mono canvas measuring 18″ × 18″
A number 18 tapestry needle

Method:

1. The entire design is worked over 2 meshes of the canvas in Upright Gobelin Stitch. Advice on how to work this stitch is given in Chapter 1.

2. Start in the lower right-hand corner, at a point 2″ up from bottom and in from side edge.

3. Following the chart in Figure 47, begin work where indicated by the arrow. Work in rows across, until entire chart is completed.

Photo 22: Heart Motif Pillow or Picture (#2)

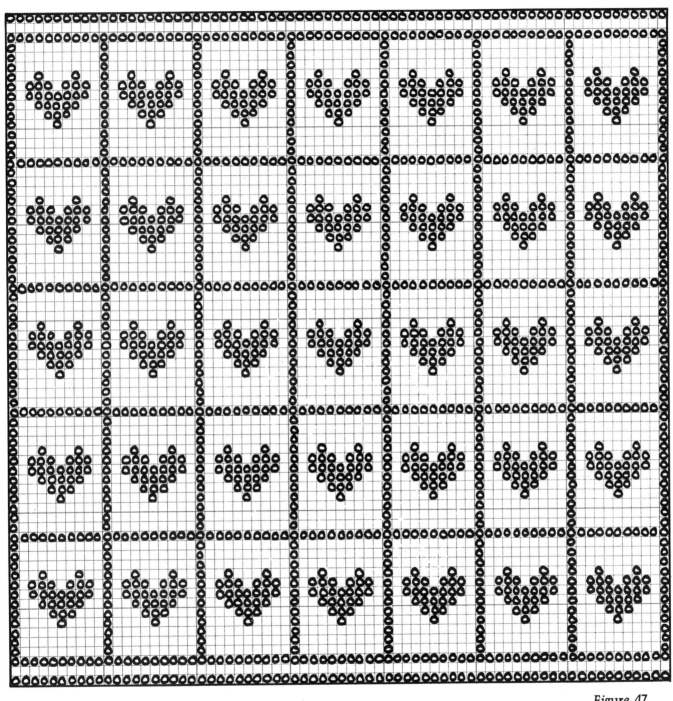

Figure 47

One square on chart = 2 stitches and 2 meshes on canvas

Unshaded squares = White

O = Red

LATCH-HOOK RUG SQUARE IN HEART MOTIF*
(Photograph 23)

Finished size: Approx. 16″ × 16″

You need: Pre cut Rug Wool
6 1-oz. units in Red
4 1-oz. units in White
A piece of 3½-mesh-to-1″ rug canvas measuring 20″ × 20″
A latch hook

Photo 23: *Latch-Hook Rug Square in Heart Motif*

Method:

1. Work the design from the lower edge upwards.
2. Start in the lower right-hand corner, at a point 2″ up from bottom and in from side edge.
3. Following the chart in Figure 48, begin work where indicated by the arrow. Work in rows across, until entire chart is completed.
4. *Do not press.*

Figure 48

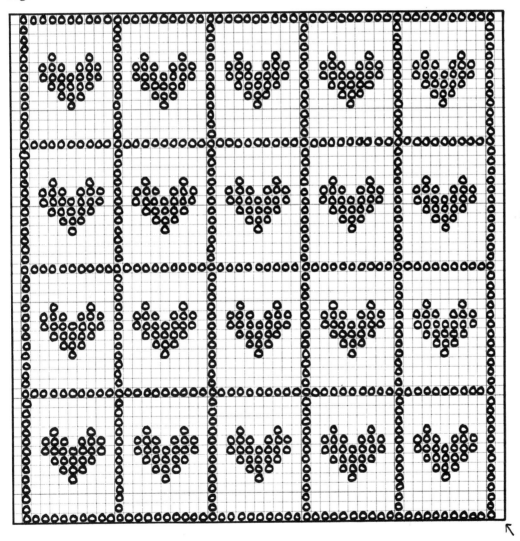

One square on
chart =
one knot on
canvas

Unshaded squares = Red
o = White

Figure 49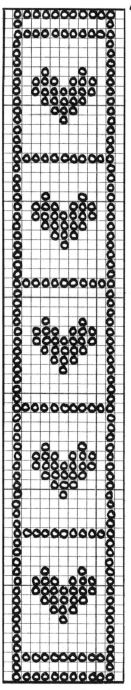

One square on chart =
4 stitches and 4 meshes
on canvas

Unshaded squares = White
O = Red

Photo 24: Cushion Strip in Heart Motif

CUSHION STRIP IN HEART MOTIF ***
(Photograph 24)

Finished size: Approx. 16″ × 3″

You need: Persian Needlepoint Wool in 10-yd. skeins
White: 3 (30 yds.)
Red: 2 (20 yds.)
A piece of 18-mesh-to-1″ mono canvas measuring 18″ × 5″
A number 22 tapestry needle

Special Note: Strips of Gobelin Embroidery can be decoratively applied to plain fabric pillows.

Method:

1. The entire design is worked with only **2** strands of Persian yarn instead of the usual **3**. The extra strand is peeled off, starting at the center of a length and working out to the ends. The extra strands are then used in pairs as they become available.

2. The entire design is worked over 4 meshes of the canvas using Upright Gobelin Stitch.

3. Start in lower right-hand corner, at a point 1″ up from bottom and in from side edge.

4. Following the chart shown in Figure 49, begin work where indicated by the arrow. Work in rows across, until entire chart is completed.

PLACE MAT IN HEART MOTIF* (Photograph 25)

Finished size: Approx. 12½" × 10¼"

You need: Persian Needlepoint Wool in 10-yd. skeins
Black: 6 (60 yds.)
Red: 3 (30 yds.)
A rectangular piece of plastic canvas with 7 holes to 1", measuring 13¼" × 10½"
A number 18 tapestry needle

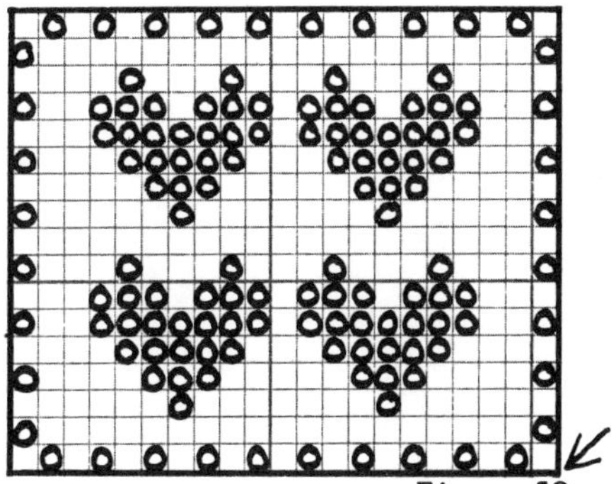

Figure 50

One square on chart =
One block of diagonal
stitches

Unshaded squares = Black
o = Red

Method:

1. The entire design is worked in blocks of the Diagonal Stitch shown in Chapter 1.

2. One square on the chart shown in Figure 50 is equivalent to 1 completed block of diagonal stitches.

3. Start in the lower right-hand corner, making sure that you work right up to the edge of the canvas (Figure 11). This will reduce the amount of trimming required at the end of work.

4. Following the chart in Figure 50, begin work where indicated by the arrow. Work in rows of blocks across, until entire chart is completed.

5. Trim away excess plastic as shown in Photograph 1.

6. Choose 1 of the colors in the design for the stitched edging. Work in an oversewing stitch from left to right as shown in Figure 12 and described in Chapter 1.

7. *Do not press.*

Photo 25: *Place Mat in Heart Motif (#1)*

PLACE MAT IN HEART MOTIF* (Figure 51)

Finished size: Approx. 12½″ × 9½″

You need: Persian Needlepoint Wool in 10-yd. skeins
White: 6 (60 yds.)
Red: 3 (30 yds.)
A rectangular piece of plastic canvas with 7 holes to 1″ measuring 13¼″ × 10½″
A number 18 tapestry needle

Method:

1. The entire design is worked in blocks of the diagonal stitch shown in Chapter 1.

2. One square on the chart shown in Figure 51 is equivalent to 1 completed block of diagonal stitches.

3. Start in the lower right-hand corner, making sure that you work right up to the edge of the canvas (Figure 11). This will reduce the amount of trimming required at the end of work.

4. Following the chart in Figure 51, begin work where indicated by the arrow. Work in rows of blocks across, until the entire chart is completed.

5. Trim away excess plastic as shown in Photograph 1.

6. Choose 1 of the colors in the design for the stitched edging. Work in an oversewing stitch from left to right as shown in Figure 12 and described in Chapter 1.

7. *Do not press.*

Figure 51

One square on chart =
one block of diagonal
stitches

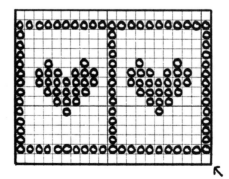

Unshaded squares = White
0 = Red

A knitted afghan and cushion, with a handsome pair of pillows or pictures worked in Upright Gobelin Stitch, are provided in this striking diamond pattern. Should you wish to expand the range of projects, please consult Chapter 1 for suggestions on how to create your own designs.

DIAMOND DAZZLER COORDINATES (Plate 6)

DIAMOND DAZZLER AFGHAN* (Photograph 26)

Finished size: Approx. 42″ × 67″ (exclusive of fringes)

You need: 4-ply acrylic or knitting worsted yarn
5 4-oz. skeins in Winter White (shade A), represented on the chart by unshaded squares.
4 4-oz. skeins in Orange (shade B), represented on the chart by black circles.
A size 10½ circular knitting needle

Gauge: 4 sts. and 5 rows to 1″ over plain st. st. on size 10½ needles

To Make: With size 10½ circular needle and shade A, cast on 159 sts.

IMPORTANT: The afghan is worked back and forth in the usual method for two needles. The circular needle is used only to make it easier to cope with the large number of stitches.

ROW 1: K

ROW 2: K3, P to within last 3 sts., K3
Repeat rows 1 and 2 until 10 rows of st.st. have been worked in shade A, join shade B.

Begin working the chart shown in Figure 52 where indicated by the black arrow.

Continue alternating bands 1 and 2 until Band 1 has been worked for the fifteenth time.

IMPORTANT: Keep a border of 3 sts. in K at either side of work throughout. This border of 3 sts. *is not* shown on the chart. Finish by working 10 rows in st. st. in shade A, bind off.

FINISHING: Weave any loose ends along the back of the work, and give the afghan a press, following the instructions given in Chapter 1.

FRINGES: Cut four 12″ lengths of yarn in shade B for each fringe, and follow the instructions given in Chapter 1 for making fringes. Space the fringes close together along upper and lower edge of the afghan, and trim the ends even, when fringing is completed.

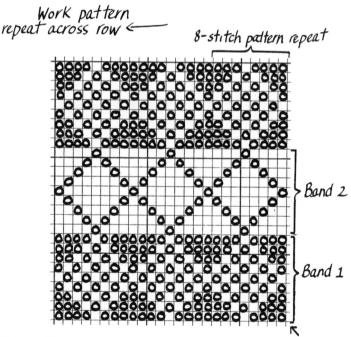

Figure 52

KNITTED CUSHION SQUARE IN DIAMOND DAZZLER* (Photograph 26)

Finished size: Approx. 16″ × 16″

Please note: You may well have sufficient yarn left over from the afghan to make the cushion cover. However, if you want to make it as a separate item, your amounts are given below. You will have enough yarn to make both sides of the cushion knitted, or you may prefer to back the knitting with a fabric in a matching or toning color.

You need: 4-ply acrylic or knitting worsted yarn
    1 4-oz. skein in Winter White (shade A), represented on the chart by unshaded squares
    1 4-oz. skein in Orange (shade B), represented on the chart by black circles.
    A pair of size 7 needles

Gauge: 4½ sts. and 6 rows to 1″ over plain st. st. on size 7 needles

Photo 26: Diamond Dazzler Afghan and Cushion Square

To Make: With size 7 needles and shade A, cast on 73 sts. Work 4 rows in st. st., join shade B. Begin working the chart shown in Figure 53, where indicated by the black arrow. When chart has been completed, work 4 more rows in st. st. in shade A, bind off.

FINISHING: Weave all the loose ends along the back of the work, and give the cushion square a press, following the instructions given in Chapter 1. Instructions for making squares into cushions will also be found in the same chapter.

Continue working
Bands 1 and 2 until
Band 1 has been
worked 5 times

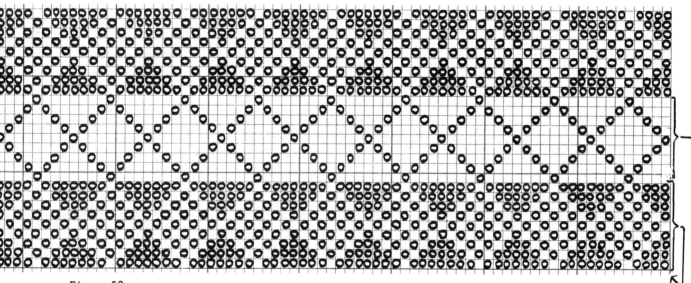

Figure 53

Band 1

Band 2

DIAMOND DAZZLER PILLOW OR PICTURE*
(Photograph 27)

Finished size: Approx. 14″ × 14″

You need: Persian Needlepoint Wool in 10-yd.
skeins
Winter White: 8 (80 yds.)
Orange: 8 (80 yds.)
A piece of 10-mesh-to-1″ mono canvas
measuring 18″ × 18″
A number 18 tapestry needle

Method:

1. The entire design is worked over 4 meshes of the canvas
   in Upright Gobelin Stitch.

2. Start in the lower right-hand corner, at a point 2″ up
   from bottom and in from side edge.

3. Following the chart in Figure 54, begin work where indicated by the arrow. Work in rows across, until entire
   chart is completed.

Unshaded squares = Winter White
0 = Orange

One square on chart = 4 stitches and 4 meshes on canvas

Photo 27: *Diamond Dazzler
Pillow or Picture (#1)*

Figure 54

DIAMOND DAZZLER PILLOW OR PICTURE**
(Photograph 28)

Finished size: ·Approx. 14″ × 14″

You need: Persian Needlepoint Wool in 10-yd. skeins
Winter White: 8 (80 yds.)
Orange: 7 (70 yds.)
A piece of 10-mesh-to-1″ mono canvas measuring 18″ × 18″
A number 18 tapestry needle

Method:

1. The entire design is worked over 2 meshes of the canvas in Upright Gobelin Stitch. Advice on how to work this stitch is given in Chapter 1.
2. Start in the lower right-hand corner, at a point 2″ up from bottom and in from side edge.
3. Following the chart in Figure 55, begin work where indicated by the arrow. Work in rows across, until entire chart is completed.

Photo 28: Diamond Dazzler Pillow or Picture (#2)

One square on chart = 2 stitches and 2 meshes on canvas
Unshaded squares = Winter White
O = Orange

Figure 55

DIAMONDS AND STRIPES COORDINATES (Plate 7)

A basically simple pattern such as this one can be varied considerably by changing the ground shade from light to dark and vice versa, thereby creating quite different but subtly coordinated results.

Full instructions are given for a knitted afghan and cushion, two pillow or picture squares worked in Upright Gobelin Stitch, a decorative cushion strip, and two place mats worked in plastic canvas. Should you wish to make additional items such as a latch-hook rug, please consult Chapter 1 for general instructions on how to create your own designs.

DIAMONDS AND STRIPES AFGHAN*
(Photograph 29)

Finished size: Approx. 44″ × 67″ (exclusive of fringe)

You need: 4-ply acrylic or knitting worsted yarn
5 4-oz. skeins in Medium Gold (shade A), represented on the chart by unshaded squares
3 4-oz. skeins in Light Gold (shade B), represented on the chart by black circles
A size 10½ circular knitting needle

Gauge: 4 sts. and 5 rows to 1″ over plain st.st. on size 10½ needles

To Make: With size 10½ circular needle and shade A, cast on 163 sts.

IMPORTANT: The afghan is worked back and forth in the usual method for two needles. The circular needle is used only to make it easier to cope with the large number of stitches.

ROW 1: K

ROW 2: K3, P to within last 3 sts., K3.
Repeat rows 1 and 2 until 18 rows in st. st. have been worked in shade A, join shade B.
Begin working the chart shown in Figure 56 where indicated by the black arrow.
Continue alternating bands 1 and 2 until Band 1 has been worked for the sixteenth time.

IMPORTANT: Keep a border of 3 sts. in K at either side of work throughout. This border of 3 sts. *is not* shown on the chart. Finish by working 18 rows in st.st. in shade A, bind off.

FINISHING: Weave any loose ends along the back of the work, and give the afghan a press, following the instructions given in Chapter 1.

FRINGES: Cut four 12″ lengths of yarn in shade B for each fringe, and follow the instructions given in Chapter 1 for making fringes. Space the fringes close together along upper and lower edge of afghan, and trim the ends even, when fringing is completed.

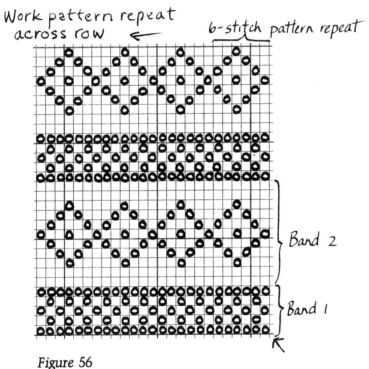

Figure 56

KNITTED CUSHION SQUARE IN DIAMONDS AND STRIPES* (Photograph 29)

Finished size: Approx. 16″ × 16″

You need: 4-ply acrylic or knitting worsted yarn
1 4-oz. skein in Medium Gold (shade A) represented on the chart by unshaded squares
1 4-oz. skein in Dark Gold (shade B), represented on the chart by black circles
A pair of size 7 needles

Photo 29: Afghan, Knitted Cushion Square in Diamonds and Stripes

Special Note: You will have enough yarn to make both sides of the cushion in knitting if you prefer this to a backing fabric.

Gauge: 4½ sts. and 6 rows to 1″ over plain st.st. on size 7 needles

To Make: With size 7 needles and shade A, cast on 73 sts. Work 2 rows in st.st., join shade B.
Begin working the chart shown in Figure 57 where indicated by the black arrow.
When chart has been completed, work 2 more rows in st.st. in shade A, bind off.

FINISHING: Weave all the loose ends along the back of the work, and give the cushion square a press, following the instructions given in Chapter 1. Instructions for making squares into cushions will also be found in the same chapter.

Continue working Bands 1 and 2 until Band 1 has been worked 6 times

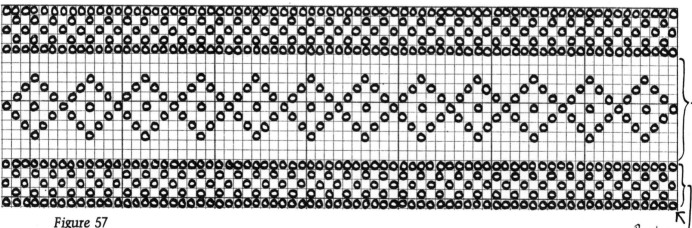

Figure 57

Band 1

Band 2

DIAMONDS AND STRIPES PILLOW OR PICTURE* (not pictured)

Finished size: Approx. 16″ × 16″

You need: Persian Needlepoint Wool in 10-yd. skeins
Dark Gold: 10 (100 yds.)
Light Gold: 6 (60 yds.)
A piece of 10-mesh-to-1″ mono canvas measuring 20″ × 20″
A number 18 tapestry needle

Method:

1. The entire design is worked over 4 meshes of the canvas in Upright Gobelin Stitch.

2. Start in the lower right-hand corner, at a point 2″ up from bottom and in from side edge.

3. Following the chart in Figure 58, begin work where indicated by the arrow. Work in rows across, until entire chart is completed.

Figure 58

One square on chart =
   4 stitches and 4 meshes
                on canvas

Unshaded squares =
       Dark Gold
     0 =
     Light Gold

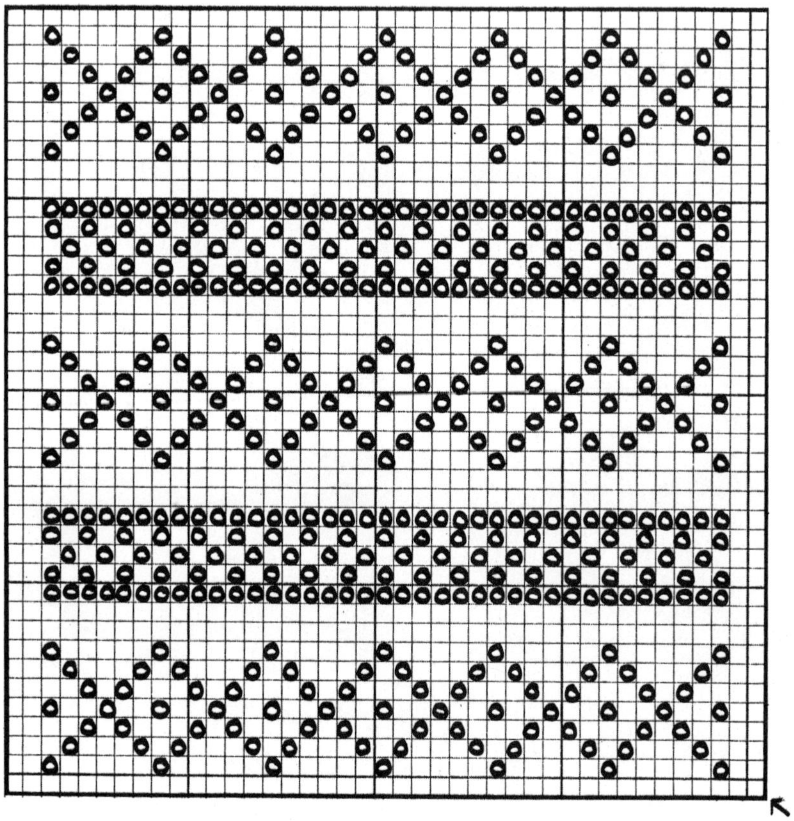

DIAMONDS AND STRIPES PILLOW OR PICTURE** (Photograph 30)

Finished size: Approx. 14″ × 14″

You need: Persian Needlepoint Wool in 10-yd. skeins
Bright Gold: 9 (90 yds.)
Dark Gold: 6 (60 yds.)
A piece of 10-mesh-to-1″ mono canvas measuring 18″ × 18″
A number 18 tapestry needle.

Method:

1. The entire design is worked over 2 meshes of the canvas in Upright Gobelin Stitch. Advice on how to work this stitch is given in Chapter 1.

2. Start in the lower right-hand corner, at a point 2″ up from bottom and in from side edge.

3. Following the chart in Figure 59, begin work where indicated by the arrow. Work in rows across, until entire chart is completed.

Photo 30: Diamonds and Stripes Pillow or Picture (#2)

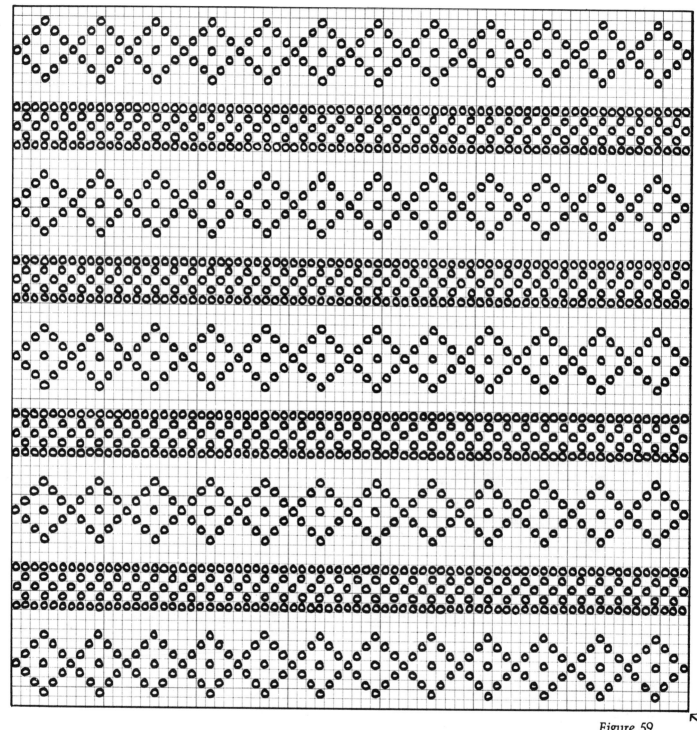

Figure 59

One square on chart = 4 stitches and 4 meshes on canvas

Unshaded squares = Bright Gold
O = Dark Gold

DIAMONDS AND STRIPES CUSHION STRIP***
(Photograph 31)

Finished size: Approx. 16″ × 3″

You need: Persian Needlepoint Wool in 10-yd. skeins
Bright Gold: 3 (30 yds.)
Dark Gold: 2 (20 yds.)
A piece of 18-mesh-to-1″ mono canvas measuring 18″ × 5″
A number 22 tapestry needle

Special Note: Strips of Gobelin Embroidery can be decoratively applied to plain fabric pillows.

Method:

1. The entire design is worked with only **2** strands of Persian yarn instead of the usual **3**. The extra strand is peeled off, starting at the center of a length and working out to the ends. The extra strands are then used in pairs as they become available.

2. The entire design is worked over 4 meshes of the canvas, using Upright Gobelin Stitch.

3. Start in lower right-hand corner, at a point 1″ up from bottom and in from side edge.

4. Following the chart shown in Figure 60 begin work where indicated by the arrow. Work in rows across, until entire chart is completed.

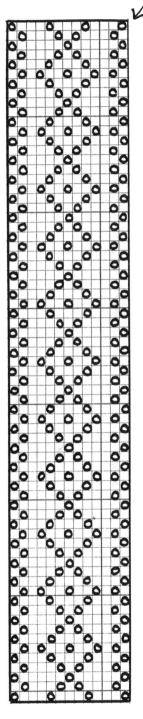

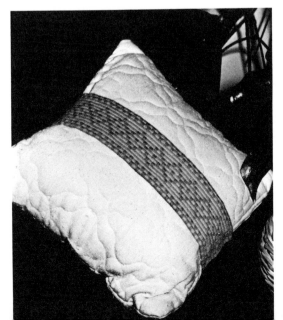

Photo 31: Diamonds and Stripes Cushion Strip

One square on chart =
4 stitches and 4 meshes
on canvas

Unshaded squares =
Bright Gold
o = Dark Gold

Figure 60

DIAMONDS AND STRIPES PLACE MAT
(Photograph 32)

Finished size: Approx. 12½″ × 10¼″

You need: Persian Needlepoint Wool in 10-yd. skeins
Bright Gold: 5 (50 yds.)
Dark Gold: 5 (50 yds.)
A rectangular piece of plastic canvas with 7 holes to 1″, measuring 13¼″ × 10½″
A number 18 tapestry needle

One square on chart = One block of diagonal stitches

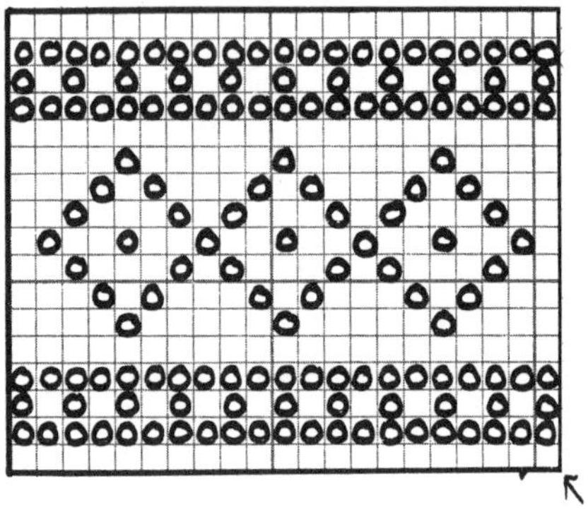

Unshaded squares = Bright Gold
o = Dark Gold

Figure 61

Method:

1. The entire design is worked in blocks of the Diagonal Stitch shown in Chapter 1.

2. One square on the chart shown in Figure 61 is equivalent to 1 completed block of diagonal stitches.

3. Start in the lower right-hand corner, making sure that you work right up to the edge of the canvas (Figure 11). This will reduce the amount of trimming required at the end of work.

4. Following the chart in Figure 61, begin work where indicated by the arrow. Work in rows of blocks across, until entire chart is completed.

5. Trim away excess plastic as shown in Photograph 1.

6. Choose 1 of the colors in the design for the stitched edging. Work in an oversewing stitch from left to right as shown in Figure 12 and described in Chapter 1.

7. *Do not press.*

Photo 32: Diamonds and Stripes Place Mat (#1)

Plate 1. Scandinavian
Rose Coordinates

Plate 2.
Windblown
Snowflakes
Coordinates

Plate 3. Enclosed Flowers Coordinates

Plate 4. Fleur-de-Lys
Coordinates

Plate 5. Heart Motif Coordinates

Plate 6. Diamond Dazzler Coordinates

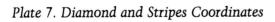

Plate 7. Diamond and Stripes Coordinates

*Plate 8. Twin
Snowflakes
Pillow
or Picture*

Plate 10. Crocheted Afghan
in Chevron Pattern

Plate 11. Patchwork
in Brick Pattern

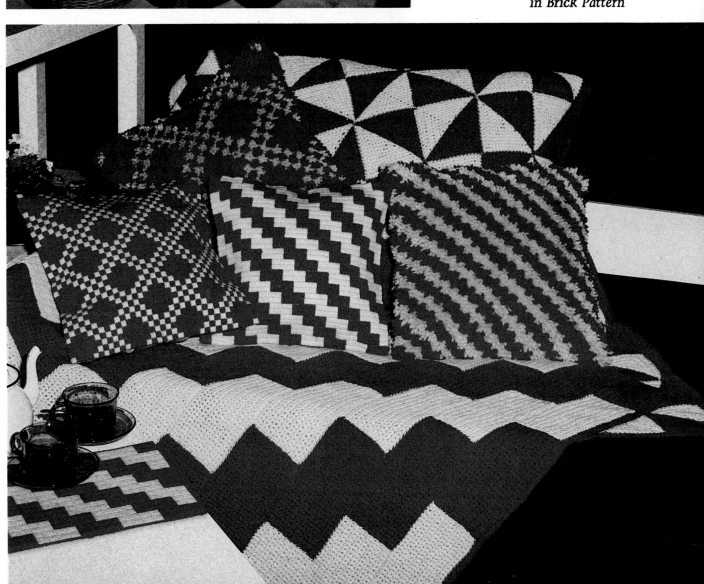

Plate 12. Patchwork
Coordinates
in Diamond-Wheel
Pattern

Plate 13. Patchwork
Coordinates
in Triangles

Plate 16. Coordinates in African Stripes

DIAMONDS AND STRIPES PLACE MAT
(Photograph 33)

Finished size: Approx. 12½″ × 10¼″

You need: Persian Needlepoint Wool in 10-yd. skeins
Bright Gold: 5 (50 yds.)
Dark Gold: 4 (40 yds.)
A rectangular piece of plastic canvas with 7 holes to 1″, measuring 13¼″ × 10½″
A number 18 tapestry needle

Method:

1. The entire design is worked in blocks of the Diagonal Stitch shown in Chapter 1.

2. One square on the chart shown in Figure 62 is equivalent to 1 completed block of diagonal stitches.

3. Start in the lower right-hand corner, making sure that you work right up to the edge of the canvas (Figure 11). This will reduce the amount of trimming required at the end of work.

4. Following the chart in Figure 62, begin work where indicated by the arrow. Work in rows of blocks across, until entire chart is completed.

5. Trim away excess plastic as shown in Photograph 1.

6. Choose 1 of the colors in the design for the stitched edging. Work in an oversewing stitch from left to right as shown in Figure 12 and described in Chapter 1.

7. *Do not press.*

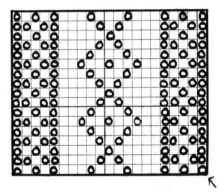

One square on chart = 4 stitches and 4 meshes on canvas

Unshaded squares = Bright Gold
○ = Dark Gold

Figure 62

Photo 33: *Diamonds and Stripes Place Mat (#2)*

COORDINATING CANVASES WITH A SCANDINAVIAN THEME

The canvas designs which follow in this section can be made into pillows or pictures which will coordinate well with the Scandinavian patterns which have been more thoroughly explored at the beginning of this chapter. Additional designs are given for table mats to be worked on rectangles of plastic canvas. The color schemes given for each pattern are only suggestions, and will, of course, depend upon your final choice to suit your own color themes and those of the items you wish to blend with them.

Should you wish to create knitted afgans and pillows, or rugs from these basic designs, please consult the general instructions for making your own designs, which can be found in Chapter 1.

One square on chart = 6 stitches and 6 meshes on canvas

Unshaded squares = Winter White
0 = Beige
X = Gray
/ = Dark Brown
• = Medium Brown

Figure 63

SNOWFLAKE MEDALLION PILLOW OR PICTURE* (not pictured)

Finished size: Approx. 16″ × 16″

You Need: Persian Needlepoint Wool in 10-yd skeins.
Winter White: 8 (80 yds.)
Beige: 4 (40 yds.)
Dark Brown: 4 (40 yds.)
Medium Brown: 4 (40 yds.)
Gray: 2 (20 yds.)
A piece of 10-mesh-to-1″ mono canvas measuring 20″ × 20″
A number 18 tapestry needle

Method:

1. The entire design is worked over 6 meshes of the canvas in Upright Gobelin Stitch.

2. Start in the lower right-hand corner, at a point 2″ up from bottom and in from side edge.

3. Following the chart in Figure 63, begin work where indicated by the arrow. Works in rows across until entire chart is completed.

TABLE MAT IN STARS* (not pictured)

Finished size: Approx. 12½″ × 10¼″

You need: Persian Needlepoint Wool in 10-yd. skeins
Dark Blue: 6 (60 yds.)
Light Blue: 4 (40 yds.)
A rectangular piece of plastic canvas with 7 holes to 1″, measuring 13¼″ × 10½″
A number 18 tapestry needle

Method:

1. The entire design is worked in blocks of the Diagonal Stitch shown in Chapter 1.

2. One square on the chart shown in Figure 64 is equivalent to 1 completed block of diagonal stitches.

3. Start in the lower right-hand corner, making sure that you work right up to the edge of the canvas (Figure 11). This will reduce the amount of trimming required at the end of work.

4. Following the chart in Figure 64, begin work where indicated by the arrow. Work in rows of blocks across, until entire chart is completed.

5. Trim away excess plastic as shown in Photograph 1.

6. Choose 1 of the colors in the design for the stitched edging. Work in an oversewing stitch from left to right as shown in Figure 12, and described in Chapter 1.

7. *Do not press.*

One square on chart =
One block of diagonal
stitches

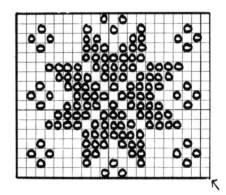

Unshaded squares =
Light Blue

Figure 64   o
Dark Blue

ROSETTE MOTIF TABLE MAT* (not pictured)

Finished size: Approx. 12½″ × 10¼″

You need: Persian Needlepoint Wool in 10-yd.
skeins
Brown: 6 (60 yds.)
Winter White: 6 (60 yds.)
A rectangular piece of plastic canvas with 7
holes to 1″, measuring 13¼″ ×
10½″
A number 18 tapestry needle

Method:

1. The entire design is worked in blocks of the Diagonal Stitch shown in Chapter 1.

2. One square on the chart shown in Figure 65, is equivalent to 1 completed block of diagonal stitches.

3. Start in the lower right-hand corner, making sure that you work right up to the edge of the canvas (Figure 11). This will reduce the amount of trimming required at the end of work.

4. Following the chart in Figure 65, begin work where indicated by the arrow. Work in rows of blocks across, until entire chart is completed.

5. Trim away excess plastic as shown in Photograph 1.

6. Choose 1 of the colors in the design for the stitched edging. Work in an oversewing stitch from left to right as shown in Figure 12 and described in Chapter 1.

7. *Do not press.*

One square on chart =
One block of diagonal
stitches

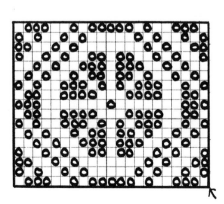

Figure 65

Unshaded squares =
Winter White
0 = Brown

TWIN SNOWFLAKES PILLOW OR PICTURE**
(Plate 8)

Finished size: Approx. 16″ × 16″

You need: Persian Needlepoint Wool in 10-yd. skeins
Black: 10 (100 yds.)
White: 5 (50 yds.)
Red: 2 (20 yds.)
A piece of 10-mesh-to-1″ mono canvas measuring 20″ × 20″
A number 18 tapestry needle

Method:

1. The entire design is worked over 4 meshes of the canvas in Upright Gobelin Stitch.

2. Start in the lower right-hand corner, at a point 2″ up from bottom and in from side edge.

3. Following the chart in Figure 66, begin work where indicated by the arrow. Work in rows across, until entire chart is completed.

One square on chart =
4 stitches and 4 meshes
on canvas

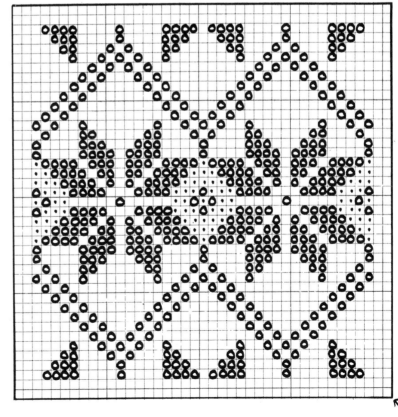

Unshaded squares = Black
O = White
· = Red

Figure 66

SNOWFLAKE TABLE MAT* (not pictured)

Finished size: Approx. 12½″ × 10¼″

You need: Persian Needlepoint Wool in 10-yd. skeins
Red: 6 (60 yds.)
White: 6 (60 yds.)
A rectangular piece of plastic canvas with 7 holes to 1″ measuring 13¼″ × 10½″
A number 18 tapestry needle

Method:

1. The entire design is worked in blocks of the Diagonal Stitch shown in Chapter 1.

2. One square on the chart shown in Figure 67, is equivalent to 1 completed block of diagonal stitches.

3. Start in the lower right-hand corner, making sure that you work right up to the edge of the canvas (Figure 11). This will reduce the amount of trimming required at the end of work.

4. Following the chart in Figure 67, begin work where indicated by the arrow. Work in rows of blocks across, until entire chart is completed.

5. Trim away excess plastic as shown in Photograph 1.

6. Choose 1 of the colors in the design for the stitched edging. Work in an oversewing stitch from left to right as shown in Figure 12, and described in Chapter 1.

7. *Do not press.*

One square on chart = One block of diagonal stitches

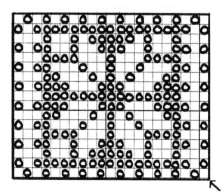

Unshaded squares = Red
O = White

Figure 67

PILLOW OR PICTURE WITH SCANDINAVIAN MEDALLION** (Plate 9)

Finished size: Approx. 14″ × 14″

You need: Persian Needlepoint Wool in 10-yd. skeins
Winter White: 10 (100 yds.)
Black: 3 (30 yds.)
Rust: 2 (20 yds.)
Beige: 1 (10 yds.)
A piece of 10-mesh-to-1″ mono canvas measuring 18″ × 18″
A number 18 tapestry needle

Method:

1. The entire design is worked over 4 meshes of the canvas in Upright Gobelin Stitch.

2. Start in the lower right-hand corner, at a point 2″ up from bottom and in from side edge.

3. Following the chart in Figure 68, begin work where indicated by the arrow. Work in rows across, until entire chart is completed.

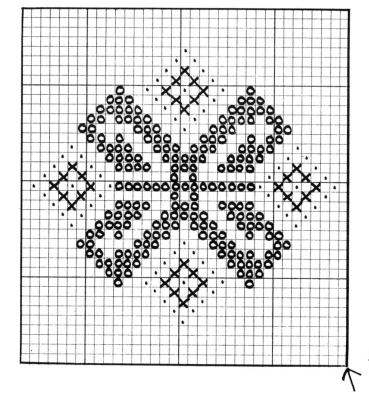

One square on chart =
4 stitches and 4 meshes
on canvas

Unshaded squares = Winter White
O = Black
• = Rust
X = Beige

Figure 68

PILLOW OR PICTURE IN BORDERED ROSETTES*
(Photograph 34)

Finished size: Approx. 16″ × 16″

You need: Persian Needlepoint Wool in 10-yd. skeins
   Brown: 9 (90 yds.)
   Winter White: 6 (60 yds.)
   Beige: 5 (50 yds.)
   A piece of 10-mesh-to-1″ mono canvas measuring 20″ × 20″
   A number 18 tapestry needle

One square on chart =
4 stitches and 4 meshes
on canvas

Figure 69

Unshaded squares = Brown
0 = Winter White
· = Beige

Method:

1. The entire design is worked over 4 meshes of the canvas in Upright Gobelin Stitch.

2. Start in the lower right-hand corner, at a point 2″ up from bottom and in from side edge.

3. Following the chart in Figure 69, begin work where indicated by the arrow. Work in rows across, until entire chart is completed.

Photo 34: Pillow or Picture in Bordered Rosettes

PILLOW OR PICTURE IN DECORATED ROSE MEDALLIONS* (Photograph 36)

Finished size: Approx. 16″ × 16″

You need: Persian Needlepoint Wool in 10-yd. skeins
Winter White: 10 (100 yds.)
Brown: 7 (70 yds.)
Copper: 3 (30 yds.)
A piece of 10-mesh-to-1″ mono canvas measuring 20″ × 20″
A number 18 tapestry needle

Photo 36:   Pillow or Picture in Decorated Rose Medallions

Method:

1. The entire design is worked over 4 meshes of the canvas in Upright Gobelin Stitch.

2. Start in the lower right-hand corner, at a point 2″ up from bottom and in from side edge.

3. Following the chart in Figure 71, begin work where indicated by the arrow. Work in rows across, until entire chart is completed.

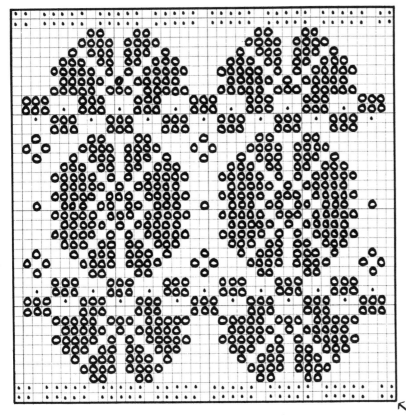

One square on chart =
4 stitches and 4 meshes
on canvas

Figure 71

Unshaded squares = Winter White
o = Brown
· = Copper

PLACE MAT IN DECORATED ROSE MEDALLION MOTIF* (not pictured)

Finished size: Approx. 12½″ × 10¼″

You need: Persian Needlepoint Wool in 10-yd. skeins
Brown: 6 (60 yds.)
Winter White: 5 (50 yds.)
A rectangular piece of plastic canvas with 7 holes to 1″ measuring 13¼″ × 10½″
A number 18 tapestry needle

Method:

1. The entire design is worked in blocks of the Diagonal Stitch shown in Chapter 1.

2. One square on the chart shown in Figure 72 is equivalent to completed block of diagonal stitches.

3. Start in the lower right-hand corner, making sure that you work right up to the edge of the canvas (Figure 11). This will reduce the amount of trimming required at the end of work.

4. Following the chart in Figure 72, begin work where indicated by the arrow. Work in rows of blocks across, until entire chart is completed.

5. Trim away excess plastic as shown in Photograph 1.

6. Choose 1 of the colors in the design for the stitched edging. Work in an oversewing stitch from left to right as shown in Figure 12 and described in Chapter 1.

7. *Do not press.*

One square on chart =
One block of diagonal
stitches

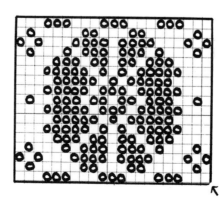

Figure 72

Unshaded squares = Winter White
0 = Brown

PLACE MAT IN DIAMONDS AND SQUARES* (not pictured)

Finished size: Approx. 12½" × 10¼"

You need: Persian Needlepoint Wool in 10-yd. skeins
Fuchsia: 5 (50 yds.)
Dusty Pink: 4 (40 yds.)
Magenta: 2 (20 yds.)
A rectangular piece of plastic canvas with 7 holes to 1", measuring 13¼" × 10½"
A number 18 tapestry needle

Method:

1. The entire design is worked in blocks of the Diagonal Stitch shown in Chapter 1.

2. One square on the chart shown in Figure 73 is equivalent to 1 completed block of diagonal stitches.

3. Start in the lower right-hand corner, making sure that you work right up to the edge of the canvas (Figure 11). This will reduce the amount of trimming required at the end of work.

4. Following the chart in Figure 73, begin work where indicated by the arrow. Work in rows of blocks across, until entire chart is completed.

5. Trim away excess plastic as shown in Photograph 1.

6. Choose 1 of the colors in the design for the stitched edging. Work in an oversewing stitch from left to right as shown in Figure 12, and described in Chapter 1.

7. *Do not press.*

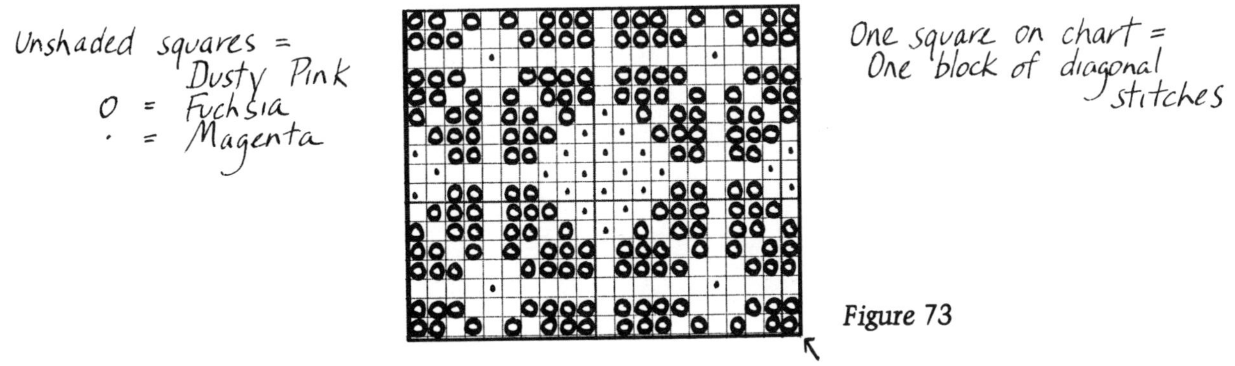

Unshaded squares =
Dusty Pink
O = Fuchsia
· = Magenta

One square on chart =
One block of diagonal
stitches

Figure 73

PILLOW OR PICTURE IN SCANDINAVIAN STRIPES (Photograph 37)

Finished size: Approx. 16″ × 16″

You need: Persian Needlepoint Wool in 10-yd. skeins
Winter White: 7 (70 yds.)
Chocolate Brown: 4 (40 yds.)
Medium Brown: 4 (40 yds.)
Copper: 2 (20 yds.)
A piece of 10-mesh-to-1″ mono canvas measuring 20″ × 20″
A number 18 tapestry needle

Photo 37: Pillow or Picture in Scandinavian Stripes

Method:

1. The entire design is worked over 4 meshes of the canvas in Upright Gobelin Stitch.

2. Start in the lower right-hand corner, at a point 2″ up from bottom and in from side edge.

3. Following the chart in Figure 74, begin work where indicated by the arrow. Work in rows across, until entire chart is completed.

One square on chart =
4 stitches and 4 meshes
on canvas

Figure 74

Unshaded squares = Winter White
X = Copper
O = Chocolate Brown
• = Medium Brown

PLACE MAT IN SCANDINAVIAN STRIPES*
(not pictured)

Finished size: Approx. 12½″ × 10¼″

You need: Persian Needlepoint Wool in 10-yd. skeins
Winter White: 5 (50 yds.)
Copper: 4 (40 yds.)
Chocolate Brown: 3 (30 yds.)
A rectangular piece of plastic canvas with 7 holes to 1″, measuring 13¼″ × 10½″
A number 18 tapestry needle

Method:

1. The entire design is worked in blocks of the Diagonal Stitch shown in Chapter 1.

2. One square on the chart shown in Figure 75 is equivalent to 1 completed block of diagonal stitches.

3. Start in the lower right-hand corner, making sure that you work right up to the edge of the canvas (Figure 11). This will reduce the amount of trimming required at the end of work.

4. Following the chart in Figure 75, begin work where indicated by the arrow. Work in rows of blocks across, until entire chart is completed.

5. Trim away excess plastic as shown in Photograph 1.

6. Choose 1 of the colors in the design for the stitched edging. Work in an oversewing stitch from left to right as shown in Figure 12, and described in Chapter 1.

7. *Do not press.*

One square on chart = one block of diagonal stitches

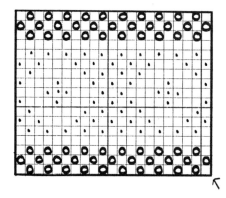

Figure 75

Unshaded squares = Winter White
o = Chocolate Brown
. = Copper

PILLOW OR PICTURE WITH DECORATED BORDER PATTERN* (Photograph 38)

Finished size: Approx. 16″ × 16″

You need: Persian Needlepoint Wool in 10-yd. skeins
Black: 10 (100 yds.)
White: 9 (90 yds.)
A piece of 10-mesh-to-1″ mono canvas measuring 20″ × 20″
A number 18 tapestry needle

Method:

1. The entire design is worked over 4 meshes of the canvas in Upright Gobelin Stitch.

2. Start in the lower right-hand corner, at a point 2″ up from bottom and in from side edge.

3. Following the chart in Figure 76, begin work where indicated by the arrow. Work in rows across, until entire chart is completed.

Photo 38: Pillow or Picture with Decorated Borders

One square on chart =
4 stitches and 4 meshes
on canvas

Unshaded squares = White
O = Black

Figure 76

PILLOW OR PICTURE IN TRELLIS OF ROSES**
(Photograph 39)

Finished size: ·Approx. 16″ × 16″

You need: Persian Needlepoint Wool in 10-yd. skeins
Black: 14 (140 yds.)
White: 6 (60 yds.)
A piece of 10-mesh-to-1″ mono canvas measuring 20″ × 20″
A number 18 tapestry needle

Method:

1. The entire design is worked over 4 meshes of the canvas in Upright Gobelin Stitch.

2. Start in the lower right-hand corner, at a point 2″ up from bottom and in from side edge.

3. Following the chart in Figure 77, begin work where indicated by the arrow. Work in rows across, until entire chart is completed.

Figure 77

One square on chart =
4 stitches and 4 meshes
on canvas

Unshaded squares = White
o = Black

PLACE MAT IN TRELLIS OF ROSES**
(Photograph 40)

Finished size: Approx. 12½″ × 10¼″

You need: Persian Needlepoint Wool in 10-yd. skeins
White: 5 (50 yds.)
Black: 5 (50 yds.)
A rectangular piece of plastic canvas with 7 holes to 1″, measuring 13¼″ × 10½″
A number 18 tapestry needle

Figure 78

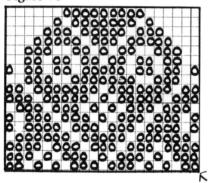

One square on chart =
One block of diagonal
stitches

Unshaded squares = White
O = Black

Method:

1. The entire design is worked in blocks of the Diagonal Stitch shown in Chapter 1.

2. One square on the chart shown in Figure 78, is equivalent to 1 completed block of diagonal stitches.

3. Start in the lower right-hand corner, making sure that you work right up to the edge of the canvas (Figure 11). This will reduce the amount of trimming required at the end of work.

4. Following the chart in Figure 78, begin work where indicated by the arrow. Work in rows of blocks across, until entire chart is completed.

5. Trim away excess plastic as shown in Photograph 1.

6. Choose 1 of the colors in the design for the stitched edging. Work in an oversewing stitch from left to right as shown in Figure 12, and described in Chapter 1.

7. *Do not press.*

*Photo 40: Place Mat in Trellis
of Roses*

PLACE MAT IN TRELLIS PATTERN**
(Photograph 41)

Finished size: Approx. 12½″ × 10¼″

You need: Persian Needlepoint Wool in 10-yd. skeins
Red: 6 (60 yds.)
White: 4 (40 yds.)
A rectangular piece of plastic canvas with 7 holes to 1″, measuring 13¼″ × 10½″
A number 18 tapestry needle

Method:

1. The entire design is worked in blocks of the Diagonal Stitch shown in Chapter 1.

2. One square on the chart shown in Figure 79, is equivalent to 1 completed block of diagonal stitches.

3. Start in the lower right-hand corner, making sure that you work right up to the edge of the canvas (Figure 11). This will reduce the amount of trimming required at the end of work.

4. Following the chart in Figure 79, begin work where indicated by the arrow. Work in rows of blocks across, until entire chart is completed.

5. Trim away excess plastic as shown in Photograph 1.

6. Choose 1 of the colors in the design for the stitched edging. Work in an oversewing stitch from left to right as shown in Figure 12, and described in Chapter 1.

7. *Do not press.*

Figure 79

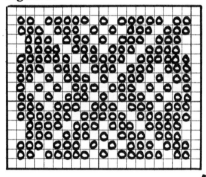

One square on chart =
One block of diagonal stitches

Unshaded squares = White
O = Red

Photo 41: *Place Mat in Trellis Pattern*

PLACE MAT IN ROSE PETAL MOTIF*
(Photograph 42)

Finished size: Approx. 12½″ × 10¼″

You need: Persian Needlepoint Wool in 10-yd. skeins
White: 6 (60 yds.)
Red: 5 (50 yds.)
A rectangular piece of plastic canvas with 7 holes to 1″, measuring 13¼″ × 10½″
A number 18 tapestry needle

One square on chart =
One block of diagonal stitches

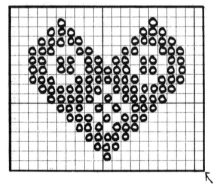

Unshaded squares = White
O = Red

Figure 80

Method:

1. The entire design is worked in blocks of the Diagonal Stitch shown in Chapter 1.

2. One square on the chart shown in Figure 80, is equivalent to 1 completed block of diagonal stitches.

3. Start in the lower right-hand corner, making sure that you work right up to the edge of the canvas (Figure 11). This will reduce the amount of trimming required at the end of work.

4. Following the chart in Figure 80, begin work where indicated by the arrow. Work in rows of blocks across, until entire chart is completed.

5. Trim away excess plastic as shown in Photograph 1.

6. Choose 1 of the colors in the design for the stitched edging. Work in an oversewing stitch from left to right as shown in Figure 12, and described in Chapter 1.

7. *Do not press.*

3 . *Patchwork Designs*

Patchwork patterns remain extremely popular as a design source for crafts today. The afghans in this section are all crocheted, but the squares and rectangles could just as easily be knitted by anyone prepared to do some calculations with graph paper and a tape measure. The beauty of working any project in small pieces, which are afterwards sewn together, is that you can easily carry your work around with you, and do a few rows in any spare time you might have during the day.

When sewing the patches together, lay out the entire design, piece by piece, on a flat surface, where it can remain undisturbed while you are working on it. Make sure the pieces are all running in the same direction, with the foundation chain at the bottom edge of each patch. This will give a better look to the finished item. Sew the patches together using an oversewing stitch, picking up the pieces from your layout as you require them.

The same patchwork designs are used for rug and canvas work. Designs can be mixed and matched as the patchwork motifs will always look well together. Additional projects appear for this purpose at the end of the chapter.

Canvas squares can be sewn together to make rugs or wall-hangings, or used as they are for cushions or pictures.

The Persian Needlepoint Wool used for most of the canvas work may be changed for a 4-ply-weight yarn. This will reduce costs, and produce an exact match for the yarns used in the crocheted projects. Approximate yardages are given for each item.

PATCHWORK IN CHEVRON PATTERNS

CROCHETED AFGHAN IN CHEVRON PATTERN*

See **Plate 10** for color illustration of the afghan with its coordinating items, and Photograph 43 for a more detailed look at the afghan itself.

Finished size: Approx. 38″ × 54″

You need:
4-ply yarn
3 4-oz. skeins in multicolored Grays/Browns (shade A)
3 4-oz. skeins in Medium Brown (shade B)
3 4-oz. skeins in Winter White (shade C)
3 4-oz. skeins in Gray (shade D)
A size I aluminum crochet hook

Gauge: 6 sts. and 7 rows to 2″ over sc using a size I hook

The Afghan: Figure 81 shows the layout of the square patches which make up this simple chevron pattern.

The Patch: Ch 15.

ROW 1: Starting in 2nd ch from hook, work 1 sc in each ch across (14 sts.), ch 1, turn.

ROW 2: 1 sc in each sc across, ch 1, turn.
Repeat Row 2 until 16 rows have been completed, fasten off.

MAKE:
30 in shade A.
29 in shade B.
29 in shade C.
29 in shade D.

TO FINISH: Sew the patches together as shown in Figure 81.

EDGING: With shade D and a size I hook, join yarn at bottom left-hand corner about 1″ along lower edge.
Work 1 sc in each foundation ch to next corner, 3 sc in corner to turn.
Work 1 sc in each row up side of work to next corner, 3 sc in corner to turn.

A	D	C	B	A	B	C	D	A
D	C	B	A	D	A	B	C	D
C	B	A	D	C	D	A	B	C
B	A	D	C	B	C	D	A	B
A	D	C	B	A	B	C	D	A
D	C	B	A	D	A	B	C	D
C	B	A	D	C	D	A	B	C
B	A	D	C	B	C	D	A	B
A	D	C	B	A	B	C	D	A
D	C	B	A	D	A	B	C	D
C	B	A	D	C	D	A	B	C
B	A	D	C	B	C	D	A	B
A	D	C	B	A	B	C	D	A

Figure 81

Photo 43: Crocheted Afghan in Chevron Pattern

Work 1 sc in each sc across top to next corner, 3 sc in corner to turn.

Work 1 sc in each row down side of work to next corner, 3 sc in corner to turn. Work along foundation chain in sc until the first stitch is reached, sl st in top of first st, ch 1.

ROW 2: Work 1 sc in each sc around, and 3 sc in center of 3 sc at each corner, join with sl st to first sc and fasten off.

GOBELIN PILLOW IN CHEVRON PATTERN*
(Photograph 44)

Finished size: Approx. 14″ × 14″

You need: 4-ply yarn
40 yds. in multicolored Grays/Browns
  (shade A)
40 yds. in Medium Brown   (shade B)
40 yds. in Winter White   (shade C)
40 yds. in Gray   (shade D)
A piece of 10-mesh-to-1″ mono canvas
  measuring 18″ × 18″
A number 18 tapestry needle

*Photo 44:   Gobelin Pillow in
Chevron Pattern*

Method:

1. The entire design is worked over 4 meshes of the canvas in Upright Gobelin Stitch.

2. Start in the lower right-hand corner, at a point 2″ up from bottom and in from side edge.

3. Following the chart in Figure 82, begin work where indicated by the arrow. Work in rows across, until entire chart is completed.

One square on chart =
4 stitches and 4 meshes
on canvas

Figure 82

Unshaded squares = Winter White
O = Gray
. = Multicolored Grays/Browns
X = Medium Brown

TABLE MAT IN CHEVRON PATTERN*
(Photograph 45)

Finished size: Approx. 12½″ × 10¼″

You need: 4-ply yarn
25 yds. in multicolored Grays/Browns
(shade A)
25 yds. in Medium Brown   (shade B)
25 yds. in Winter White   (shade C)
25 yds. in Gray   (shade D)
A rectangular piece of plastic canvas with 7
holes to 1″, measuring 13¼″ × 10½″
A number 18 tapestry needle

Method:

1. The entire design is worked in blocks of the Diagonal Stitch shown in Chapter 1.

2. One square on the chart shown in Figure 83 is equivalent to 1 completed block of diagonal stitches.

3. Start in the lower right-hand corner, making sure that you work right up to the edge of the canvas (Figure 11). This will reduce the amount of trimming required at the end of work.

4. Following the chart in Figure 83, begin work where indicated by the arrow. Work in rows of blocks across, until entire chart is completed.

5. Trim away excess plastic as shown in Photograph 1.

6. Choose 1 of the colors in the design for the stitched edging. Work in an oversewing stitch from left to right as shown in Figure 12, and described in Chapter 1.

7. *Do not press.*

Photo 45: Table Mat in Chevron Pattern

Figure 83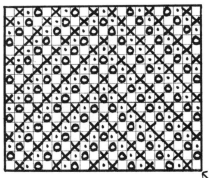

One square on chart =
One block of diagonal
stitches

Unshaded squares = Winter White
O = Gray
. = Multicolored Grays/Browns
X = Medium Brown

LATCH-HOOK RUG SQUARE IN CHEVRON PATTERN* (Photograph 46)

Finished size: Approx. 16″ × 16″

You need: Precut Rug Wool
5 1-oz. units in Winter White
   (shade A)
3 1-oz. units in Gray   (shade B)
3 1-oz. units in Medium Brown   (shade
   C)
A piece of 3½-mesh-to-1″ rug canvas measuring 20″ × 20″
A latch hook

*Photo 46: Latch-Hook Rug
Square in Chevron Pattern*

Method:

1. Work the design from the lower edge upwards.

2. Start in the lower right-hand corner, at a point 2″ up from bottom and in from side edge.

3. Following the chart in Figure 84, begin work where indicated by the arrow. Work in rows across, until entire chart is completed.

4. *Do not press.*

One square on chart = one knot on canvas

Unshaded squares = Winter White
           O = Gray
           . = Medium Brown

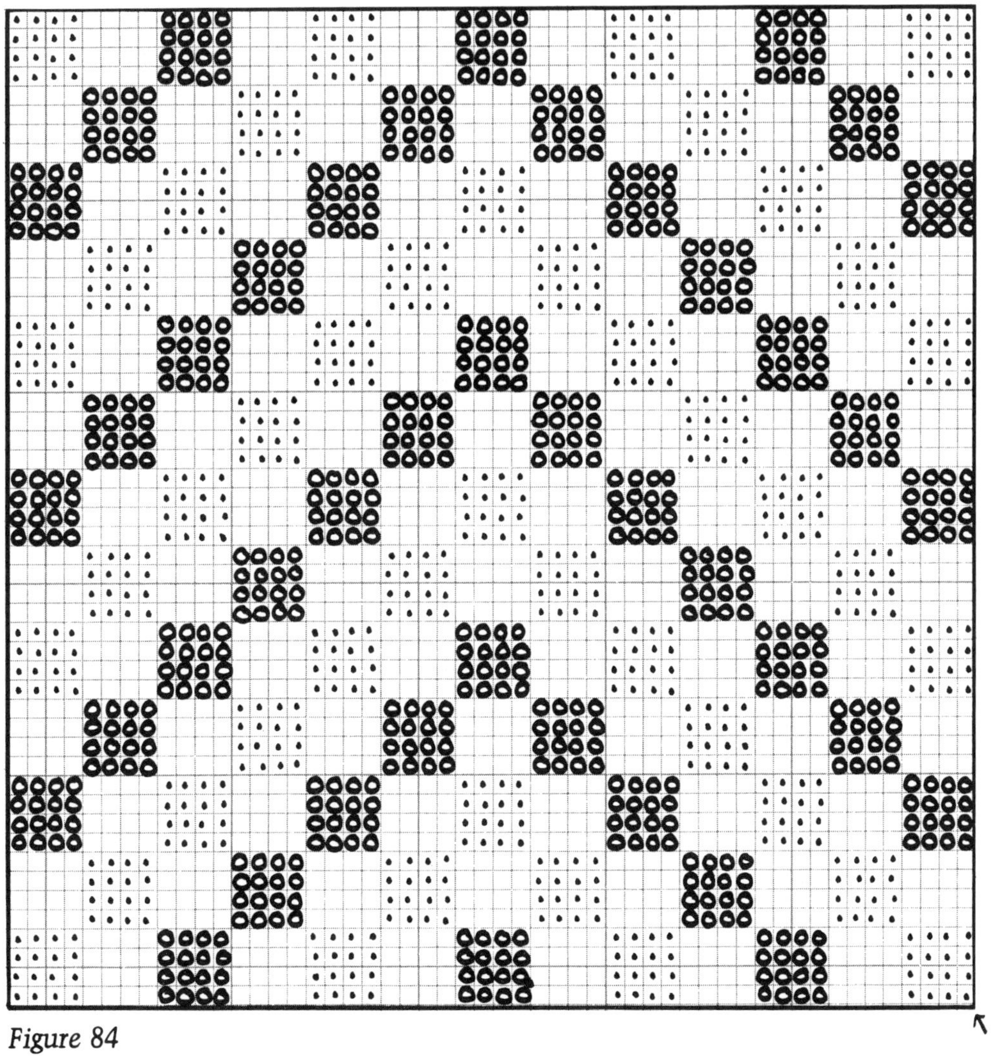

Figure 84

PATCHWORK IN BRICK PATTERN (PLATE 11)

CROCHETED AFGHAN IN BRICK PATTERN*
(Photograph 47)

Finished size: Approx. 38″ × 55″

You need: 4-ply acrylic or knitting worsted yarn
4 4-oz. skeins in Red (shade A)
4 4-oz. skeins in White (shade B)
A size I aluminum crochet hook

Gauge: 6 sts. and 7 rows to 2″ over sc using a size I hook.

The Afghan: Figure 85 shows the layout of the square and rectangular patches which make up this simple brick pattern.

The Rectangular Patch Ch 29.

ROW 1: Starting in 2nd ch from hook, work 1 sc in each ch across (28 sts.), ch 1, turn.

ROW 2: 1 sc in each sc across, ch 1, turn.
Repeat Row 2 until 16 rows have been completed, fasten off.

MAKE: 26 in shade A.
26 in shade B.

The Square Patch Ch 15.

ROW 1: Starting in 2nd ch from hook, work 1 sc in each ch across (14 sts.), ch 1, turn.

ROW 2: 1 sc in each sc across, ch 1, turn.
Repeat Row 2 until 16 rows have been completed, fasten off.

MAKE: 7 in shade A.
6 in shade B.

TO FINISH: Sew the patches together as shown in Figure 85.

EDGING: With shade A and a size I hook, join yarn at bottom left-hand corner about 1″ along lower edge.
Work 1 sc in each foundation ch to next corner, 3 sc in corner to turn.

A	B	A	B	A
B	A	B	A	B
B	A	B	A	B
A	B	A	B	A
A	B	A	B	A
B	A	B	A	B
B	A	B	A	B
A	B	A	B	A
A	B	A	B	A
B	A	B	A	B
B	A	B	A	B
A	B	A	B	A
A	B	A	B	A

Figure 85

Photo 47: Crocheted Afghan in Brick Pattern

Work 1 sc in each row up side of work to next corner, 3 sc in corner to turn.

Work 1 sc in each sc across top to next corner, 3 sc in corner to turn.

Work 1 sc in each row down side of work to next corner, 3 sc in corner to turn. Work along foundation chain in sc until the first stitch is reached, sl st in top of first st, ch 1.

ROW 2: Work 1 sc in each sc around, and 3 sc in center of 3 sc at each corner, join with a sl st to first sc and fasten off.

GOBELIN PILLOW OR PICTURE IN BRICK PATTERN* (Photograph 48)

Finished size: Approx. 14″ × 14″

You need: Persian Needlepoint Wool in 10-yd. skeins
Red: 6 (60 yds.)
White: 6 (60 yds.)
A piece of 10-mesh-to-1″ mono canvas measuring 18″ × 18″
A number 18 tapestry needle

Method:

1. The entire design is worked over 4 meshes of the canvas in Upright Gobelin Stitch.

2. Start in the lower right-hand corner, at a point 2″ up from bottom and in from side edge.

3. Following the chart in Figure 86, begin work where indicated by the arrow. Work in rows across, until entire chart is completed.

One square on chart = 4 stitches and 4 meshes on canvas

Unshaded squares = White
O = Red

Photo 48: *Gobelin Pillow or Picture in Brick Pattern*

Figure 86

TABLE MAT IN BRICK PATTERN*
(Photograph 49)

Finished size: Approx. 13¼″ × 9½″

You need: Persian Needlepoint Wool in 10-yd. skeins.
Red: 5 (50 yds.)
White: 5 (50 yds.)
A rectangular piece of plastic canvas with 7 holes to 1″, measuring 13¼″ × 10½″
A number 18 tapestry needle

Method:

1. The entire design is worked in blocks of the Diagonal Stitch shown in Chapter 1.

2. One square on the chart shown in Figure 87 is equivalent to 1 completed block of diagonal stitches.

3. Start in the lower right-hand corner, making sure that you work right up to the edge of the canvas. (Figure 11). This will reduce the amount of trimming required at the end of work.

4. Following the chart in Figure 87, begin work where indicated by the arrow. Work in rows of blocks across, until entire chart is completed.

5. Trim away excess plastic as shown in Photograph 1.

6. Choose 1 of the colors in the design for the stitched edging. Work in an oversewing stitch from left to right as shown in Figure 12, and described in Chapter 1.

7. *Do not press.*

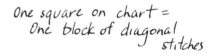

One square on chart = One block of diagonal stitches

Unshaded squares = White
0 = Red

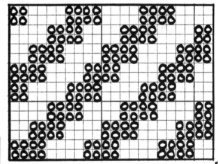

Figure 87

Photo 49: Table Mat in Brick Pattern

LATCH-HOOK RUG SQUARE IN BRICK PATTERN* (Photograph 50)

Finished size: Approx. 16″ × 16″

You need: Precut Rug Wool
5 1-oz. units in Red
5 1-oz. units in White
A piece of 3½ mesh-to-1″ rug canvas measuring 20″ × 20″
A latch hook

Photo 50:   *Latch-Hook Rug Square in Brick Pattern*

Method:

1. Work the design from the lower edge upwards.
2. Start in the lower right-hand corner, at a point 2″ up from bottom and in from side edge.
3. Following the chart in Figure 88, begin work where indicated by the arrow. Work in rows across, until entire chart is completed.
4. *Do not press.*

One square on chart = one knot on canvas

Unshaded squares = White
O = Red

Figure 88

PATCHWORK COORDINATES IN DIAMOND-WHEEL PATTERN (Plate 12)

CROCHETED AFGHAN IN DIAMOND-WHEEL PATTERN** (Photograph 51)

Finished size: Approx. 40″ × 59″

You need: 4-ply acrylic or knitting worsted yarn
6 4-oz. skeins in Red   (shade A)
6 4-oz. skeins in White   (shade B)
A size I aluminum crochet hook

Gauge: 6 sts. and 7 rows to 2″ over sc using a size I hook

The Afghan: Figure 89 shows the layout of the triangular motifs which make up the diamond pattern.

The Triangle   Ch 2.

ROW 1: Work 3 sc in 2nd ch from hook, ch 1, turn.

ROW 2: 2 sc in first sc, 3 sc in next sc, 2 sc in last sc, ch 1, turn (7 sc).

ROWS 3 AND 4: 2 sc in first sc, 1 sc in each sc to center sc, 3 sc in center sc, 1 sc in each sc to last sc, 2 sc in last sc, ch 1, turn.

ROW 5: 1 sc in each sc to center sc, 3 sc in center sc, 1 sc in each sc to end, ch 1, turn.

ROWS 6, 7 AND 8: As rows 3 and 4.

ROW 9: As Row 5, fasten off.

MAKE: 96 in shade A.
96 in shade B.

TO FINISH: Sew 1 triangle in shade A and 1 in shade B together, across the longest side, making a square from the 2 triangles. Repeat this process for all the triangles. Now sew the patches together as shown in Figure 89.

EDGING: Work 4 rounds of sc around outside edge of afghan, using shade A, and working 3 sc in each corner on every row.

Photo 51: Crocheted Afghan in Diamond-Wheel Pattern

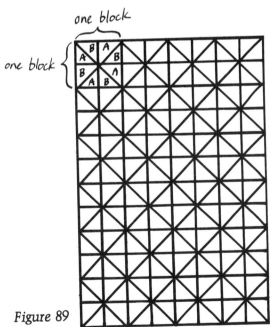

one block

one block

Figure 89

Diamonds are arranged in same color sequence for each block

GOBELIN PILLOW OR PICTURE IN DIAMOND-WHEEL PATTERN*** (Photograph 52)

Finished size: Approx. 14″ × 14″

You need: Persian Needlepoint Wool in 10-yd. skeins
Red: 8 (80 yds.)   (shade A)
White: 9 (90 yds.)   (shade B)
A piece of 10-mesh-to-1″ mono canvas measuring 18″ × 18″
A number 18 tapestry needle

Method:

1. The canvas is worked in Graduated Upright Gobelin Stitch.
2. Figure 90 shows in detail how 1 block of stitches is worked.
3. Figure 91 shows how the blocks are linked together.

Photo 52:   Gobelin Pillow or Picture in Diamond-Wheel Pattern

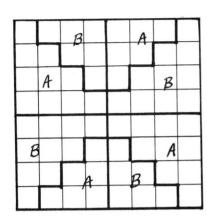

One square on chart = one stitch and one mesh
on canvas

Figure 90

one block

Figure 91

block

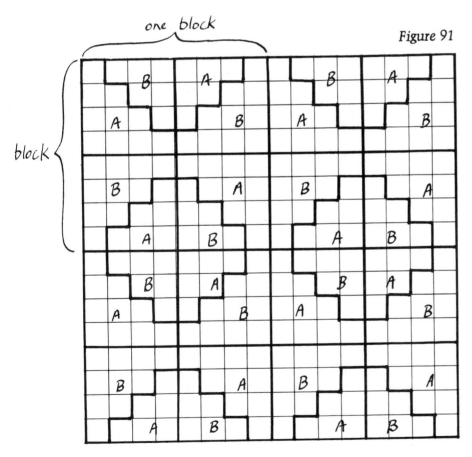

One square on chart = one stitch and one mesh
on canvas

4. Figure 92 shows the arrangement of blocks which creates the final design.

5. Start working the design in the lower right-hand corner, at a point 2″ up from bottom and in from side edge.

6. Following the charts provided, work in rows of blocks across the canvas until 18 rows have been completed.

One square on chart = one block of stitches as shown in Figure 90

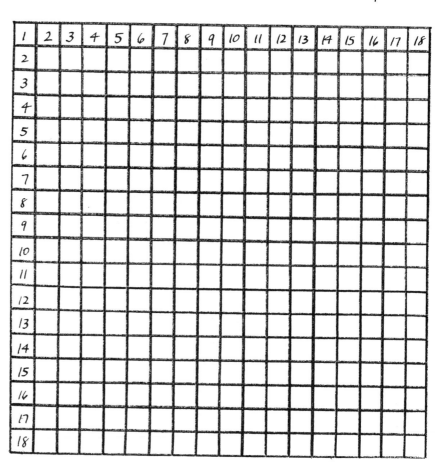

Figure 92

LATCH-HOOK RUG IN DIAMOND-WHEEL PATTERN** (Photograph 53)

Finished size: Approx. 24½″ × 72″

You need: Precut Rug Wool
34 1-oz. units in Red   (shade A)
27 1-oz. units in White   (shade B)
A piece of 3½-mesh-to-1″ rug canvas measuring 28″ × 76″
A latch hook
Rug Binding: 6 yds.

Photo 53: Latch-Hook Rug in Diamond-Wheel Pattern

1	2	3	4	5
2				
3				
4				
5				
6				
7				
8				
9				
10				
11				
12				
13				
14				
15				

One square on chart =
one block of stitches as
shown in Figure 94

Figure 93

Method:

1. The rug is made up of "blocks" of patterning. Figure 93 shows the layout of these blocks. The rug is 15 blocks long and 5 blocks wide.

2. Figure 94 shows how the first row of blocks is worked. Each subsequent row is worked in the same manner until all 15 rows of blocks are completed.

3. Work the design from the lower edge upwards.

4. Start in the lower right-hand corner, at a point 2" up from bottom and in from side edge of canvas.

5. Following the chart in Figure 94, begin work where indicated by the arrow. Work in rows across until all 15 blocks of the pattern are completed.

6. Turn under raw edges of the canvas, and bind with rug binding.

7. *Do not press.*

Figure 94

One square on chart = one knot on canvas

Chart shows one row of blocks

Work 15 rows of blocks as shown in Figure 93

one block

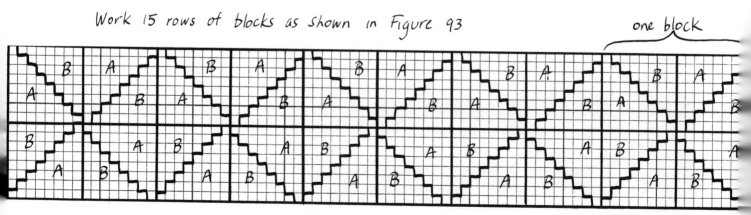

CROCHETED AFGHAN IN TRIANGLES**
(Photograph 54)

PATCHWORK COORDINATES IN TRIANGLES (Plate 13)

Finished size: Approx. 42″ × 64″

You need: 4-ply acrylic or knitting worsted yarn
3 4-oz. skeins in Beige   (shade A)
3 4-oz. skeins in Gray   (shade B)
3 4-oz. skeins in multicolored Grays/ Browns   (shade C)
3 4-oz. skeins in Medium Brown   (shade D)
A size I aluminum crochet hook

Photo 54: Crocheted Afghan in Triangles

Gauge: 6 sts. and 7 rows to 2″ over sc using a size I hook

The Afghan: Figure 95 shows the layout of the triangular motifs which make·up the overall pattern.

The Triangle   Ch 2.

ROW 1: Work 3 sc in 2nd ch from hook, ch 1, turn.

ROW 2: 2 sc in first sc, 3 sc in next sc, 2 sc in last sc, ch 1, turn (7 sc).

ROWS 3 AND 4: 2 sc in first sc, 1 sc in each sc to center sc, 3 sc in center sc, 1 sc in each sc to last sc, 2 sc in last sc, ch 1, turn.

ROW 5: 1 sc in each sc to center sc, 3 sc in center sc, 1 sc in each sc to end, ch 1, turn.

ROWS 6, 7, and 8: As rows 3 and 4.

ROW 9: As Row 5, fasten off.

MAKE: 59 in shade A.
59 in shade B.
58 in shade C.
58 in shade D.

TO FINISH: Sew 1 triangle in shade A and 1 in shade B together, across the longest side, making a square from the 2 triangles. Repeat this process for all the triangles in shades A and B. Now sew triangles in shades C and D together in the same manner. Sew the patches together as shown in Figure 95.

EDGING: Work 2 rounds of sc around outside edge of afghan, using shade D, and working 3 sc in each corner on every row. Break off shade D and join shade C.
Work 1 more round in sc, working 3 sc in each corner.
Finish by working 1 round of sc from LEFT TO RIGHT instead of the usual manner from right to left. This creates an attractive edging. Work only 1 sc in each corner.

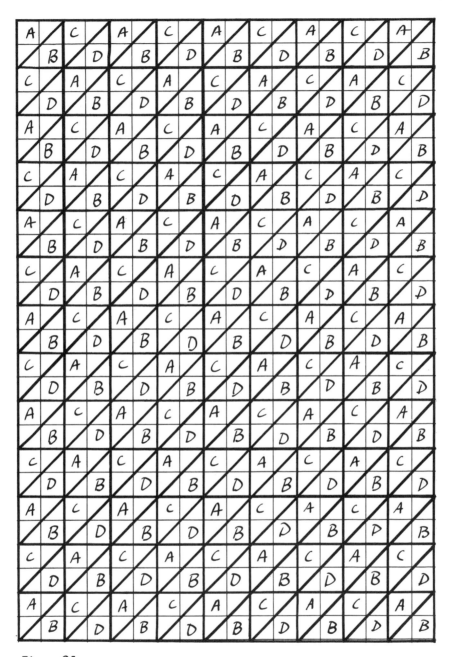

Figure 95

GOBELIN PILLOW OR PICTURE IN TRIANGLES*** (Photograph 55)

Finished size: Approx. 14″ × 14″

You need: 4-ply acrylic or knitting worsted yarn
    40 yds. in Cream (shade A)
    40 yds. in Gray (shade B)
    40 yds. in multicolored Grays/Browns (shade C)
    40 yds. in Medium Brown (shade D)
    A piece of 10-mesh-to-1 mono canvas measuring 18″ × 18″
    A number 18 tapestry needle

Method:

1. The canvas is worked in Graduated Upright Gobelin Stitch.

Photo 55: Gobelin Pillow or Picture in Triangles

2. Figure 96 shows in detail how 1 block of stitches is worked.

3. Figure 97 shows how the blocks are linked together.

4. Figure 98 shows the arrangement of blocks which creates the final design.

5. Start working the design in the lower right-hand corner, at a point 2″ up from bottom and in from side edge.

6. Following the charts provided, work in rows of blocks across the canvas until 7 rows have been completed.

One square on chart = one stitch and one mesh on canvas

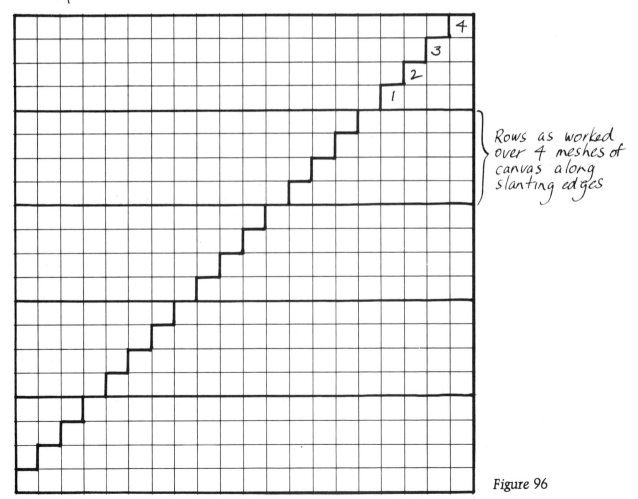

Rows as worked over 4 meshes of canvas along slanting edges

Figure 96

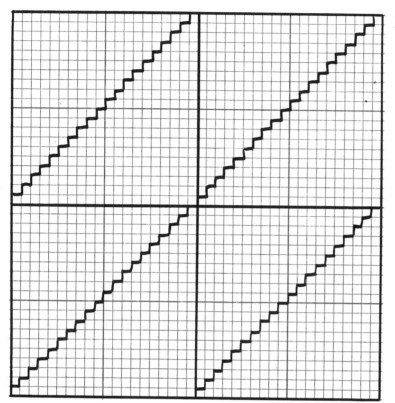

Figure 97

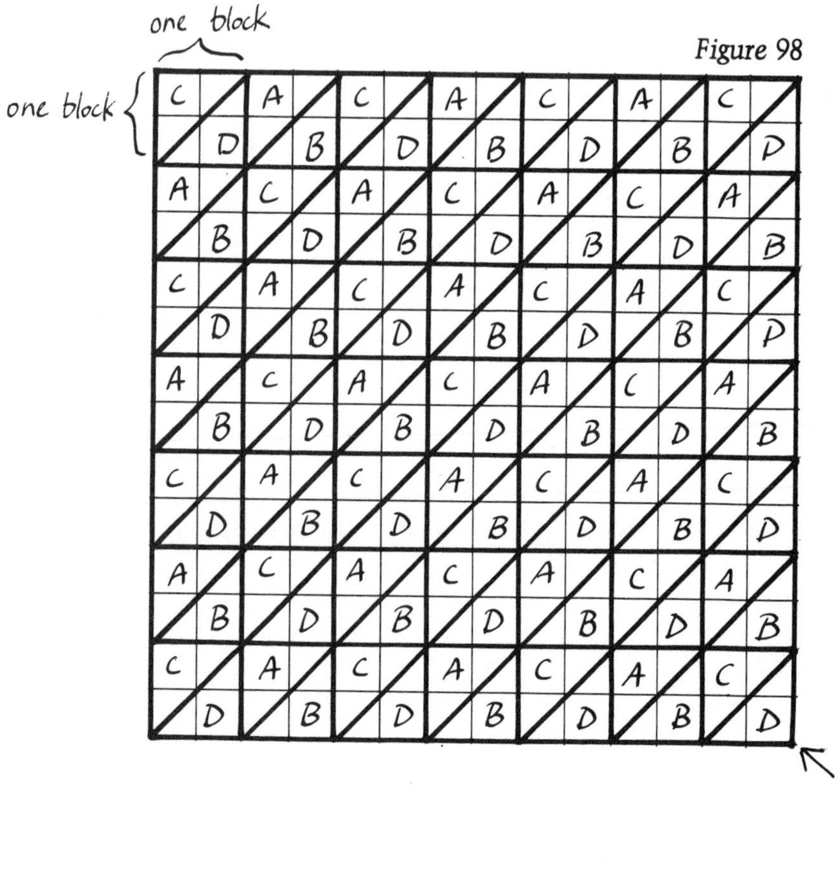

one block

one block

Figure 98

LATCH-HOOK RUG IN TRIANGLES**
(Photograph 56)

Finished size: 33″ × 33″

You need: Precut Rug Wool
    11 1-oz. units in Cream   (shade A)
    9 1-oz. units in Chocolate   (shade B)
    11 1-oz. units in Gray   (shade C)
    9 1-oz. units in Medium Brown   (shade
      D)A piece of 3½-mesh-to-1″ rug canvas
      measuring 36″ × 36″
    A latch hook
    Rug Binding: 4 yds.

Photo 56:   Latch-Hook Rug in Triangles

Method:

1. The rug is made up of 2 alternating blocks of pattern. Figure 99 shows the layout of these blocks.

   The rug is 11 blocks in each direction.

2. Figures 100 and 101 show blocks 1 and 2 of the pattern in detail.

3. Work the design from the lower edge upwards.

4. Start in the lower right-hand corner, at a point 1½″ up from bottom and in from side edge.

Figure 99

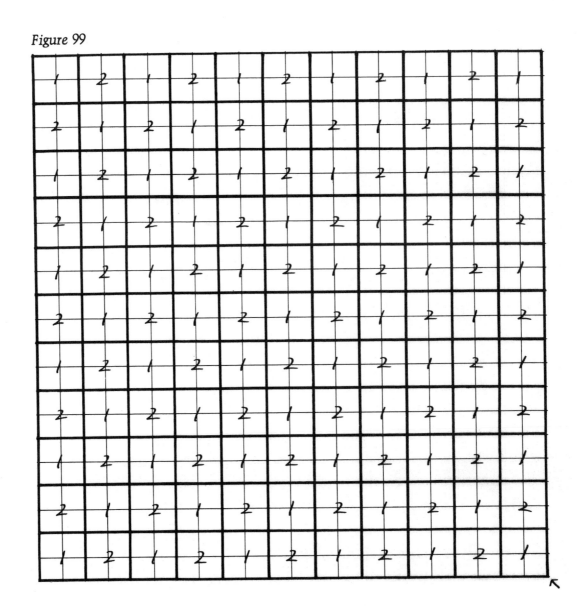

5. Following the layout chart and the detailed charts provided, begin work where indicated by the arrow. Work in rows across until all 11 blocks of pattern are completed.

6. Turn under raw edges of the canvas, and bind with rug binding.

7. *Do not press.*

Block #1

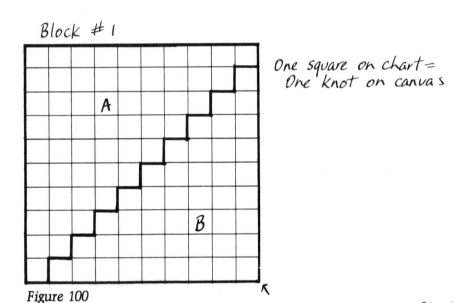

One square on chart = One knot on canvas

Figure 100

Block #2

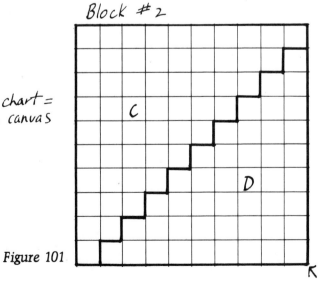

One square on chart = One knot on canvas

Figure 101

PATCHWORK COORDINATES IN RECTANGLES AND SQUARES

CROCHETED AFGHAN IN RECTANGLES AND SQUARES* (Photograph 57)

Finished size:　Approx. 42″ × 64″

You need:　　4-ply acrylic or knitting worsted yarn
7 4-oz. skeins in Beige　(shade A)
4 4-oz. skeins in Winter White　(shade B)
A size I aluminum crochet hook

Gauge: 6 sts. and 7 rows to 2″ over sc using a size I hook

Photo 57: Crocheted Afghan in Rectangles and Squares

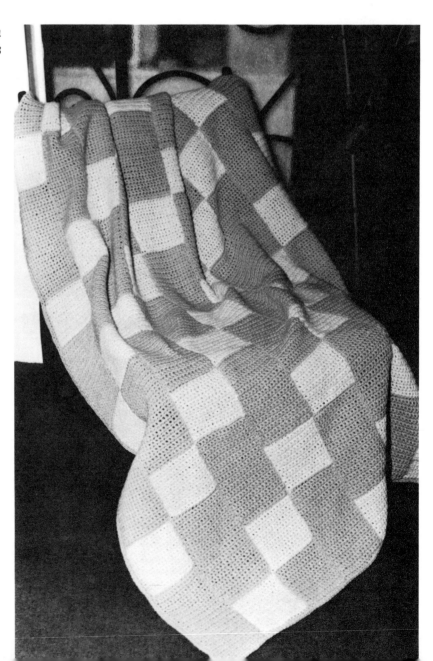

The Afghan: Figure 102 shows the layout of the square and rectangular patches which make up this simple design.

The Rectangular Patch   Ch 15.

ROW 1:Starting in 2nd ch from hook, work 1 sc in each ch across (14 sts.), ch 1, turn.

ROW 2: 1 sc in each sc across, ch 1, turn.
Repeat Row 2 until 32 rows have been completed, fasten off.

MAKE: 44 in shade A.

The Square Patch   Work as for Rectangular Patch to end of Row 2. Repeat Row 2 until 16 rows have been completed, fasten off.

MAKE: 6 in shade A.
46 in shade B.

TO FINISH: Sew the patches together as shown in Figure 102.

EDGING: With shade A and a size I hook, join yarn at bottom left-hand corner about 1″ along lower edge.
Work 1 sc in each foundation ch to next corner, 3 sc in corner to turn.
Work 1 sc in each row up side of work to next corner, 3 sc in corner to turn.
Work 1 sc in each sc across top to next corner, 3 sc in corner to turn.
Work 1 sc in each row down side of work to next corner, 3 sc in corner to turn. Work along foundation chain in sc until the first stitch is reached, sl st in top of first st, ch 1.

ROW 2:Work 1 sc in each sc around, and 3 sc in center of 3 sc at each corner, join with a sl st to first sc, fasten off.

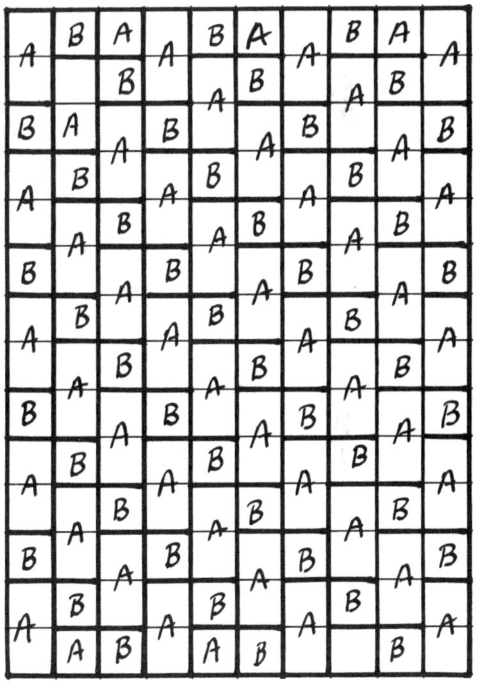

Figure 102

PLACE MAT IN RECTANGLES AND SQUARES*
(Photograph 58)

Finished size: Approx. 13¼″ × 9½″

You need: Persian Needlepoint Wool in 10-yd. skeins
Beige: 3 (30 yds.)
Winter White: 5 (50 yds.)
A rectangular piece of plastic canvas with 7 holes to 1″, measuring 13¼″ × 10½″
A number 18 tapestry needle

Method:

1. The entire design is worked in blocks of the Diagonal Stitch shown in Chapter 1.

2. One square on the chart shown in Figure 103 is equivalent to 1 completed block of diagonal stitches.

3. Start in the lower right-hand corner, making sure that you work right up to the edge of the canvas (Figure 11). This will reduce the amount of trimming required at the end of work.

4. Following the chart in Figure 103, begin work where indicated by the arrow. Work in rows of blocks across, until entire chart is completed.

5. Trim away excess plastic as shown in Photograph 1.

6. Choose 1 of the colors in the design for the stitched edging. Work in an oversewing stitch from left to right as shown in Figure 12, and described in Chapter 1.

7. *Do not press.*

Photo 58: Place Mat in
Rectangles and Squares

One square on chart = one block of diagonal
stitches

Figure 103

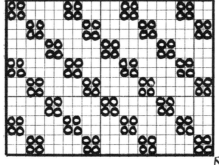

Unshaded squares =
Winter White
o =
Beige

"PATCHWORK QUILT" COORDINATES

"PATCHWORK QUILT" CROCHETED AFGHAN*
(Photograph 59)

Finished size: Approx. 40″ × 64″

You need: 4-ply acrylic or knitting worsted yarn
4 4-oz. skeins in Chocolate   (shade A)
4 4-oz. skeins in Parchment   (shade B)
2 4-oz. skeins in Beige   (shade C)
A size I aluminum crochet hook

Gauge: 6 sts. and 7 rows to 2″ over sc using a size I hook

The Afghan: Figure 104 shows the layout of the patches of this design which was based on a traditional quilt pattern.

Large Square Patch   Ch 29.

ROW 1: Starting in 2nd ch from hook, work 1 sc in each ch across (28 sts.), ch 1, turn.

ROW 2: 1 sc in each sc across, ch 1, turn.
Repeat Row 2 until 32 rows have been completed, fasten off.

MAKE: 6 in shade A.

Small Square Patch   Ch 15.

ROW 1: Starting in 2nd ch from hook, work 1 sc in each ch across (14 sts.), ch 1, turn.

ROW 2: 1 sc in each sc across, ch 1, turn.
Repeat Row 2 until 16 rows have been completed, fasten off.

MAKE: 24 in shade A.
2 in shade B.

Rectangular Patch #1   Work as for Large Square Patch to the end of Row 2.
Repeat Row 2 until 16 rows have been completed, fasten off.

MAKE: 12 in shade B.

A	#1	B	A	#4	A	#1	B	A
#2		A		#2	C	#2		A		#2
B			B		B			B
A	#1	B	A		A	#1	B	A
	#3	C		B		#3	C	
A	#1	B	A	#4	A	#1	B	A
#2		A	#2		#2		A		#2
B			B	C	B			B
A	#1	B	A		A	#1	B	A
	#3	C		B		#3	C	
A	#1	B	A	#4	A	#1	B	A
#2		A	#2		#2		A		#2
B			B	C	B			B
A	#1	B	A		A	#1	B	A

Figure 104

Rectangular Patch #2 Work as for Small Square Patch to the end of Row 2.
Repeat Row 2 until 32 rows have been completed, fasten off.

MAKE: 12 in shade B.

Rectangular Patch #3 Ch 57.

ROW 1: Starting in 2nd ch from hook, work 1 sc in each ch across (56 sts.), ch 1, turn.

ROW 2: 1 sc in each sc across, ch 1, turn.
Repeat Row 2 until 16 rows have been completed, fasten off.

MAKE: 4 in shade C.

Rectangular Patch #4 Work as for Small Square Patch to end of Row 2.
Repeat Row 2 until 64 rows have been completed, fasten off.

MAKE: 3 in shade C.

TO FINISH: Sew patches together as shown in Figure 104.

EDGING: With shade A and a size I hook, join yarn at bottom left-hand corner about 1" along lower edge.
Work 1 sc in each foundation ch to next corner, 3 sc in corner to turn.
Work 1 sc in each row up side of work to next corner, 3 sc in corner to turn.
Work 1 sc in each sc across top to next corner, 3 sc in corner to turn.
Work 1 sc in each row down side of work to next corner, 3 sc in corner to turn. Work along foundation chain in sc until the first stitch is reached, sl st in top of first st, ch 1.

ROW 2: Work 1 sc in each sc around, and 3 sc in center of 3 sc at each corner, join with a sl st to first sc and fasten off.

GOBELIN PILLOW OR PICTURE IN "PATCHWORK QUILT" PATTERN*
(Photograph 60)

Finished size: Approx. 16″ × 16″

You need: Persian Needlepoint Wool in 10-yd. skeins.
Beige: 7 (70 yds.)
Parchment: 6 (60 yds.)
Chocolate: 6 (60 yds.)
A piece of 10-mesh-to-1″ mono canvas measuring 20″ × 20″
A number 18 tapestry needle

Photo 60: Gobelin Pillow or Picture in "Patchwork Quilt" Pattern

Method:

1. The entire design is worked over 4 meshes of the canvas in Upright Gobelin Stitch.

2. Start in the lower right-hand corner, at a point 2″ up from bottom and in from side edge.

3. Following the chart in Figure 105, begin work where indicated by the arrow. Work in rows across, until entire chart is completed.

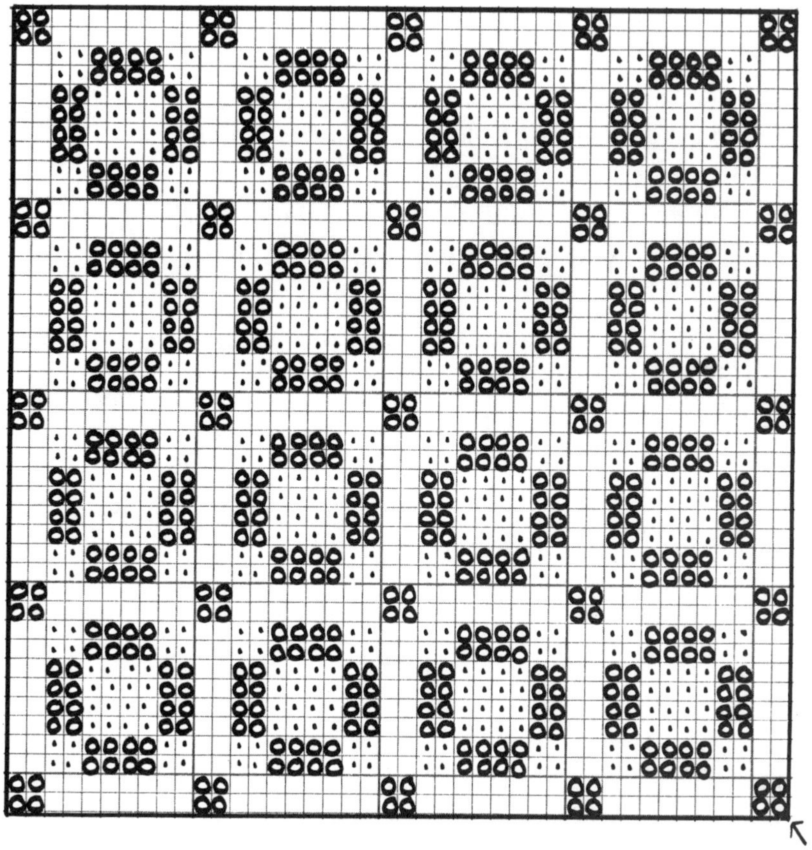

One square on chart = 4 stitches and 4 meshes on canvas

Figure 105

Unshaded squares = Beige
O = Parchment
• = Chocolate

TABLE MAT IN "PATCHWORK QUILT" PATTERN* (Photograph 61)

Finished size: Approx. 12½″ × 10¼″

You need: Persian Needlepoint Wool in 10-yd. skeins.
Beige: 4 (40 yds.)
Parchment: 3 (30 yds.)
Chocolate: 3 (30 yds.)
A rectangular piece of plastic canvas with 7 holes to 1″, measuring 13¼″ × 10″
A number 18 tapestry needle

Method:

1. The entire design is worked in blocks of the Diagonal Stitch shown in Chapter 1.

2. One square on the chart shown in Figure 106 is equivalent to 1 completed block of diagonal stitches.

3. Start in the lower right-hand corner, making sure that you work right up to the edge of the canvas (Figure 11). This will reduce the amount of trimming required at the end of work.

4. Following the chart in Figure 106, begin work where indicated by the arrow. Work in rows of blocks across, until entire chart is completed.

5. Trim away excess plastic as shown in Photograph 1.

6. Choose 1 of the colors in the design for the stitched edging. Work in an oversewing stitch from left to right as shown in Figure 12, and described in Chapter 1.

7. *Do not press.*

Photo 61: Table Mat in
"Patchwork Quilt" Pattern

one square on chart = one block of diagonal stitches

Unshaded squares = Beige
O = Chocolate
' = Parchment

Figure 106

COORDINATES IN STRIPED AND PLAIN PATCHES

CROCHETED AFGHAN IN STRIPED AND PLAIN PATCHES* (Photograph 62)

Finished size: Approx. 42″ × 64″

You need: 4-ply acrylic or knitting worsted yarn
6 4-oz. skeins in Beige (shade B)
5 4-oz. skeins in Winter White (shade A)
A size I aluminum crochet hook

Gauge: 6 sts. and 7 rows to 2″ over sc using a size I hook

The Afghan: Figure 107 shows the layout of the plain and striped patches which are assembled to complete the afghan.

The Square Patch   Ch 15.

ROW 1:Starting in 2nd ch from hook, work 1 sc in each ch across (14 sts.), ch 1, turn.

ROW 2: 1 sc in each sc across, ch 1, turn.
Repeat Row 2 until 16 rows have been completed, fasten off.

MAKE: 35 in shade A.
35 in shade B.

The Striped Rectangular Patch (make 35.)
With shade B, ch 15.
Work rows 1 and 2 as for Square Patch, do not break off shade B, but join shade A.
Work Row 2 twice in shade A.
Continue working Row 2, alternating 2 rows in shade B and 2 rows in shade A, until the eighth stripe has been worked in shade A, fasten off.

TO FINISH:Sew the patches together as shown in Figure 107.

EDGING: With shade B and a size I hook, join yarn at bottom left-hand corner about 1″ along lower edge.
Work 1 sc in each foundation ch to next corner, 3 sc in corner to turn.
Work 1 sc in each row up side of work to next corner, 3 sc in corner to turn.
Work 1 sc in each sc across top to next corner, 3 sc in corner to turn.

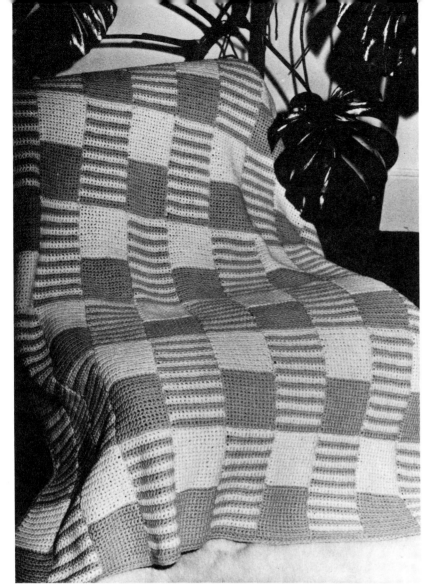

Work 1 sc in each row down side of work to next corner, 3 sc in corner to turn. Work along foundation chain in sc until the first stitch is reached, sl st in top of first st, ch 1.

ROW 2: Work 1 sc in each sc around, and 3 sc in center of 3 sc at each corner, join with a sl st to first sc and fasten off.

Figure 107

A		A		A		A		A	
B		B		B		B		B	
	A		A		A		A		A
	B		B		B		B		B
A		A		A		A		A	
B		B		B		B		B	
	A		A		A		A		A
	B		B		B		B		B
A		A		A		A		A	
B		B		B		B		B	
	A		A		A		A		A
	B		B		B		B		B
A		A		A		A		A	
B		B		B		B		B	

GOBELIN PILLOW OR PICTURE IN STRIPED AND PLAIN PATCHES** (Photograph 63)

Finished size: Approx. 14″ × 14″

You need: Persian Needlepoint Wool in 10-yd. skeins
Winter White: 6 (60 yds.)
Beige: 6 (60 yds.)
A piece of 10-mesh-to-1″ mono canvas measuring 18″ × 18″
A number 18 tapestry needle

Method:

1. The design is worked in Upright Gobelin Stitch over 4 meshes of the canvas, except for the rectangles marked "R" and the squares marked "S."

2. The rectangles and squares thus marked are worked in Upright Gobelin Stitch over 2 meshes of the canvas, following the charts shown in figures 108 and 109.

3. Start in the lower right-hand corner, at a point 2″ up from bottom and in from side edge.

4. Following the chart in Figure 110, begin work where indicated by the arrow. Work in rows across, until entire chart is completed.

Photo 63: Gobelin Pillow or Picture in Plain and Striped Patches

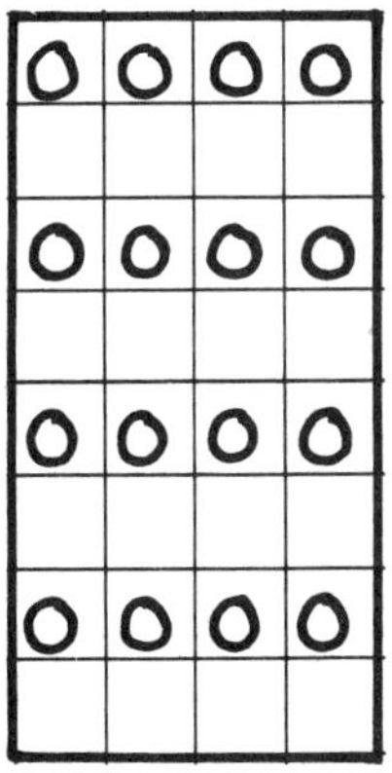

Rectangle

One square on chart = 2 stitches and 2 meshes on canvas

Unshaded squares = Beige
            O = Winter White

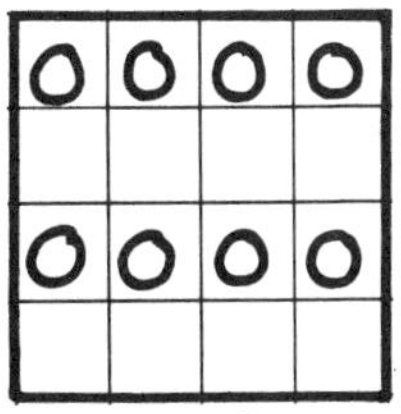

Figure 108

Square

One square on chart = 2 stitches and 2 meshes on canvas
Unshaded squares = Beige
           O = Winter White

Figure 109

One square on chart =
   4 stitches and 4 holes on canvas
  except for areas marked "R"
  and "S" for which separate
  charts appear in Figures 108
  and 109

Unshaded squares = Beige
           O = Winter White

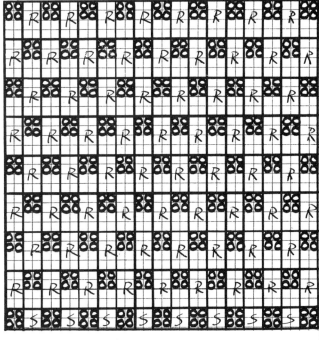

Figure 110

COORDINATING ITEMS WITH A PATCHWORK THEME

The items which follow would blend in well with the patchwork themes already developed in this chapter, and will suggest many more simple designs which you can explore and create for yourself.

A PAIR OF CUSHIONS IN DIAGONAL PATCHES
(Photograph 64)

Photo 64: Pair of Cushions in Diagonal Patches

GOBELIN PILLOW OR PICTURE IN DIAGONAL PATCHES (Photograph 65)

Finished size: Approx. 14″ × 14″

You need: Persian Needlepoint Wool in 10-yd. skeins.
Red: 9 (90 yds.)
White: 6 (60 yds.)
A piece of 10-mesh-to-1″ mono canvas measuring 18″ × 18″
A number 18 tapestry needle

Method:

1. The entire design is worked over 4 meshes of the canvas in Upright Gobelin Stitch

2. Start in the lower right-hand corner, at a point 2″ up from bottom and in from side edge.

3. Following the chart in Figure 111, begin work where indicated by the arrow. Work in rows across, until entire chart is completed.

Photo 65:   Gobelin Pillow or Picture in Diagonal Patches

One square on chart =
4 stitches and 4 meshes
on canvas

Unshaded squares = Red
O = White

Figure 111

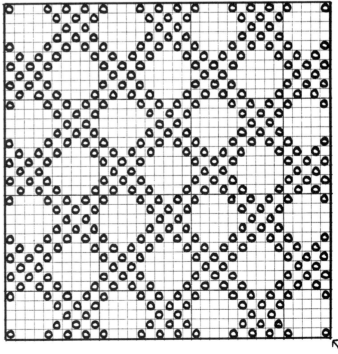

LATCH-HOOK RUG SQUARE IN DIAGONAL PATCHES* (Photograph 66)

Finished size: Approx. 16″ × 16″

You need: Precut Rug Wool
7 1-oz. units in Red
3 1-oz. units in White
A piece of 3½-mesh-to-1″ rug canvas measuring 20″ × 20″
A latch hook

Photo 66: Latch-Hook Rug in Diagonal Patches

Method:

1. Work the design from the lower edge upwards.
2. Start in the lower right-hand corner, at a point 2 '' up from bottom and in from side edge.
3. Following the chart in Figure 112, begin work where indicated by the arrow. Work in rows across, until entire chart is completed.
4. *Do not press.*

One square on chart = one knot on canvas

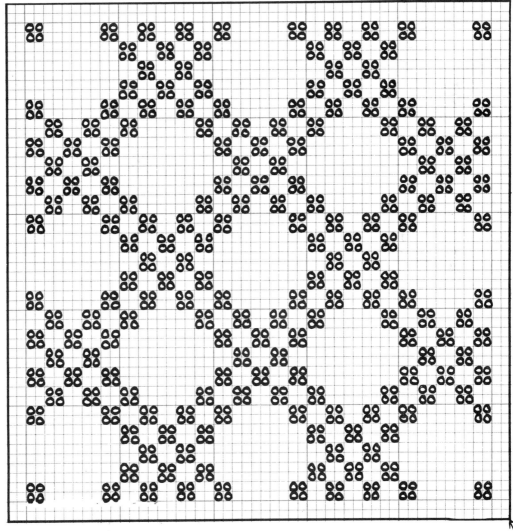

Unshaded squares = Red
O = White

Figure 112

CROCHETED FLOOR CUSHION IN SQUARE PATCHES* (Photograph 67)

Finished size: Approx. 36″ × 36″

You need: 4-ply acrylic or knitting worsted yarn
3 4-oz. skeins in Brown   (shade A)
2 4-oz. skeins in Beige   (shade B)
1 4-oz. skein in Winter White   (shade C)
A size G aluminum crochet hook
A piece of backing fabric measuring 37″ × 37″

Gauge: 8 sts. and 8½ rows to 2″ over sc using a size G hook

The Floor Cushion: Figure 113 shows the layout of squares which make up the overall pattern.

The Square   Ch 15.

ROW 1: Starting in 2nd ch from hook, work 1 sc in each ch across (14 sts.), ch 1, turn.

ROW 2: 1 sc in each sc across, ch 1, turn.
Repeat Row 2 until 16 rows have been completed, fasten off.

MAKE: 37 in shade A.
32 in shade B.
12 in shade C.

TO FINISH: Sew the patches together as shown in Figure 113. Join the crocheted square to the fabric square to make a cushion, as described in Chapter 1.

Photo 67: Crocheted Floor Cushion in Square Patches

B	A	B	A	B	A	B	A	B
A	B	A	B	A	B	A	B	A
B	A	C	A	C	A	C	A	B
A	B	A	C	B	C	A	B	A
B	A	C	B	A	B	C	A	B
A	B	A	C	B	C	A	B	A
B	A	C	A	C	A	C	A	B
A	B	A	B	A	B	A	B	A
B	A	B	A	B	A	B	A	B

Figure 113

GOBELIN PILLOW OR PICTURE IN SQUARE PATCHES* (Photograph 68)

Finished size: Approx. 14″ × 14″

You need: Persian Needlepoint Wool in 10-yd. skeins
Brown: 6 (60 yds.)
Winter White: 6 (60 yds.)
Beige: 3 (30 yds.)
A piece of 10-mesh-to-1″ mono canvas measuring 18″ × 18″
A number 18 tapestry needle

Method:

1. The entire design is worked over 4 meshes of the canvas in Upright Gobelin Stitch.
2. Start in the lower right-hand corner, at a point 2″ up from bottom and in from side edge.
3. Following the chart in Figure 114, begin work where indicated by the arrow. Work in rows across, until entire chart is completed.

Figure 114

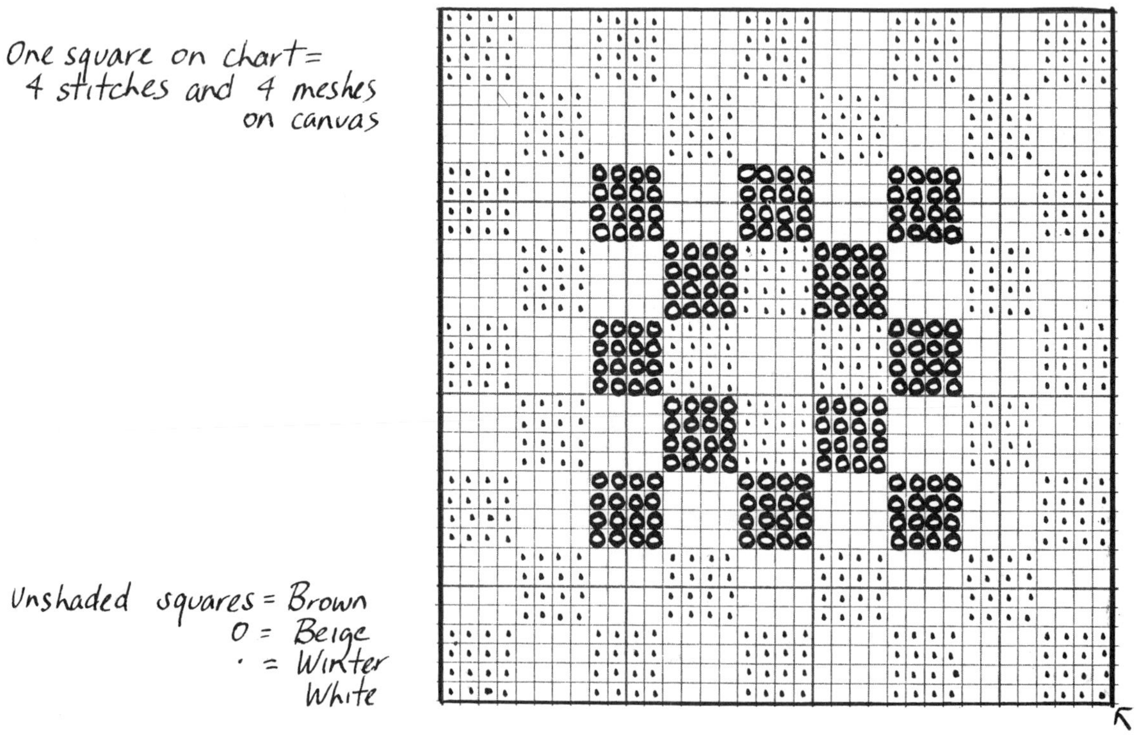

One square on chart =
4 stitches and 4 meshes
on canvas

Unshaded squares = Brown
O = Beige
· = Winter White

Photo 68: Gobelin Pillow or
Picture in Square Patches

CROCHETED FLOOR CUSHION IN CROSS PATTERN* (Photograph 69)

Finished size: Approx. 36″ × 36″

You need: 4-ply acrylic or knitting worsted yarn
3 4-oz. skeins in Gray (shade A)
2 4-oz. skeins in multicolored Grays/ Browns (shade B)
2 4-oz. skeins in Winter White (shade C)
A size G aluminum crochet hook
A piece of backing fabric measuring 37″ × 37″

Photo 69: *Crocheted Floor Cushion in Cross Pattern*

Gauge: 8 sts. and 8½ rows to 2″ over sc using a size G hook

The Floor Cushion: Figure 115 shows the layout of squares which make up the overall pattern.

The Square   Ch 15.

ROW 1: Starting in 2nd ch from hook, work 1 sc in each ch across (14 sts.), ch 1, turn.

ROW 2: 1 sc in each sc across, ch 1, turn.
Repeat Row 2 until 16 rows have been completed, fasten off.

MAKE: 40 in shade A.
        21 in shade B.
        20 in shade C.

TO FINISH: Sew the patches together as shown in Figure 115. Join the crocheted square to the fabric square to make cushion, as described in Chapter 1.

B	A	C	A	B	A	C	A	B
A	B	A	C	A	C	A	B	A
C	A	B	A	C	A	B	A	C
A	C	A	B	A	B	A	C	A
B	A	C	A	B	A	C	A	B
A	C	A	B	A	B	A	C	A
C	A	B	A	C	A	B	A	C
A	B	A	C	A	C	A	B	A
B	A	C	A	B	A	C	A	B

Figure 115

GOBELIN PILLOW OR PICTURE IN CROSS PATTERN* (Photograph 70)

Finished size: Approx. 14″ × 14″

You need: 4-ply acrylic or knitting worsted yarn
Gray: 6 (60 yds.)
multicolored Grays/Browns: 4 (40 yds.)
Winter White: 4 (40 yds.)
A piece of 10-mesh-to-1″ mono canvas measuring 18″ × 18″
A number 18 tapestry needle

Photo 70: Gobelin Pillow or Picture in Cross Pattern

Method:

1. The entire design is worked over 4 meshes of the canvas in Upright Gobelin Stitch.

2. Start in the lower right-hand corner, at a point 2″ up from bottom and in from side edge.

3. Following the chart in Figure 116, begin work where indicated by the arrow. Work in rows across, until entire chart is completed.

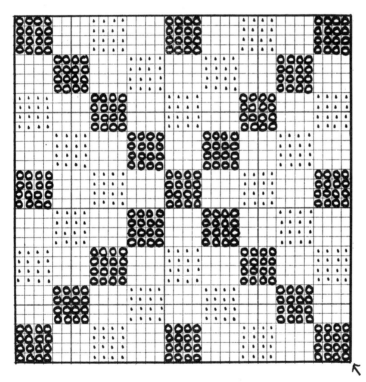

Figure 116

One square on chart = 4 stitches and 4 meshes on canvas

Unshaded squares = Gray
     O = Multicolored Grays/Browns
    · = Winter White

TABLE MAT IN CROSS PATTERN* (Photograph 71)

Finished size: Approx. 13¼″ × 9½″

You need: 4-ply acrylic or knitting worsted yarn
Gray: 4 (40 yds.)
multicolored Grays/Browns: 3 (30 yds.)
Winter White: 2 (20 yds.)
A rectangular piece of plastic canvas with 7
  holes to 1″, measuring 13¼″ × 10½″
A number 18 tapestry needle.

Method:

1. The entire design is worked in blocks of the Diagonal Stitch shown in Chapter 1.
2. One square on the chart shown in Figure 117 is equivalent to 1 completed block of diagonal stitches.
3. Start in the lower right-hand corner, making sure that you work right up to the edge of the canvas (Figure 11). This will reduce the amount of trimming required at the end of work.
4. Following the chart in Figure 117, begin work where indicated by the arrow. Work in rows of blocks across, until entire chart is completed.
5. Trim away excess plastic as shown in Photograph 1.
6. Choose 1 of the colors in the design for the stitched edging. Work in an oversewing stitch from left to right as shown in Figure 12 and described in Chapter 1.
7. *Do not press.*

One square on chart = one block of diagonal stitches

Unshaded squares = Gray
O = Multicolored Grays/Browns
· = Winter White

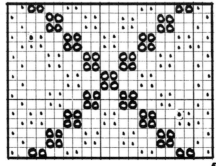

Figure 117

*Photo 71: Table Mat in Cross
Pattern*

PATCHWORK TABLE MATS

There follows a small group of Table Mat designs which will coordinate well with other items in this chapter. The possibilities are endless, the few examples given here being offered as a stimulus to create your own patterns.

TABLE MAT #1* (Figure 118)

Finished size: Approx. 13¼″ × 9½″

You need: Persian Needlepoint Wool in 10-yd. skeins
Copper: 4 (40 yds.)
Caramel: 4 (40 yds.)
Coral: 2 (20 yds.)
A rectangular piece of plastic canvas with 7 holes to 1″, measuring 13¼″ × 10½″
A number 18 tapestry needle

Figure 118

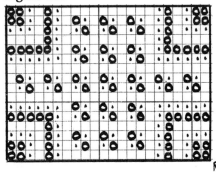

One square on chart =
one block of diagonal
stitches

Unshaded squares = Copper
0 = Coral
· = Caramel

Method:

1. The entire design is worked in blocks of the Diagonal Stitch shown in Chapter 1.

2. One square on the chart shown in Figure 118 is equivalent to 1 completed block of diagonal stitches.

3. Start in the lower right-hand corner, making sure that you work right up to the edge of the canvas (Figure 11). This will reduce the amount of trimming required at the end of work.

4. Following the chart in Figure 118, begin work where indicated by the arrow. Work in rows of blocks across, until entire chart is completed.

5. Trim away excess plastic as shown in Photograph 1.

6. Choose 1 of the colors in the design for the stitched edging. Work in an oversewing stitch from left to right as shown in Figure 12, and described in Chapter 1.

7. *Do not press.*

TABLE MAT #2* (Photograph 72)

Finished size: Approx. 12½″ × 10¼″

You need: Persian Needlepoint Wool in 10-yd. skeins
Cream: 4 (40 yds.)
Medium Brown: 3 (30 yds.)
Beige: 3 (30 yds.)
A rectangular piece of plastic canvas with 7 holes to 1″ measuring 13¼″ × 10½″
A number 18 tapestry needle

Method:

1. The entire design is worked in blocks of the Diagonal Stitch shown in Chapter 1.

2. One square on the chart shown in Figure 119 is equivalent to 1 completed block of diagonal stitches.

3. Start in the lower right-hand corner, making sure that you work right up to the edge of the canvas (Figure 11). This will reduce the amount of trimming required at the end of work.

4. Following the chart in Figure 119, begin work where indicated by the arrow. Work in rows of blocks across, until entire chart is completed.

5. Trim away excess plastic as shown in Photograph 1.

6. Choose 1 of the colors in the design for the stitched edging. Work in an oversewing stitch from left to right as shown in Figure 12, and described in Chapter 1.

7. *Do not press.*

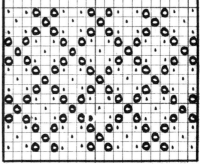

Figure 119

One square on chart =
one block of diagonal
stitches

Unshaded squares = Cream
o = Medium
Brown
· = Beige

Photo 72: Patchwork Table Mat #2

TABLE MAT #3* (Figure 120)

Finished size: Approx. 13¼″ × 9½″

You need: Persian Needlepoint Wool in 10-yd. skeins.
Black: 3 (30 yds.)
Red: 3 (30 yds.)
White: 2 (20 yds.)
A rectangular piece of plastic canvas with 7 holes to 1″, measuring 13¼″ × 10½″
A number 18 tapestry needle

Method:

1. The entire design is worked in blocks of the Diagonal Stitch shown in Chapter 1.

2. One square on the chart shown in Figure 120 is equivalent to 1 completed block of diagonal stitches.

3. Start in the lower right-hand corner, making sure that you work right up to the edge of the canvas (Figure 11). This will reduce the amount of trimming required at the end of work.

4. Following the chart in Figure 120, begin work where indicated by the arrow. Work in rows of blocks across, until entire chart is completed.

5. Trim away excess plastic as shown in Photograph 1.

6. Choose 1 of the colors in the design for the stitched edging. Work in an oversewing stitch from left to right as shown in Figure 12, and described in Chapter 1.

7. *Do not press.*

Figure 120

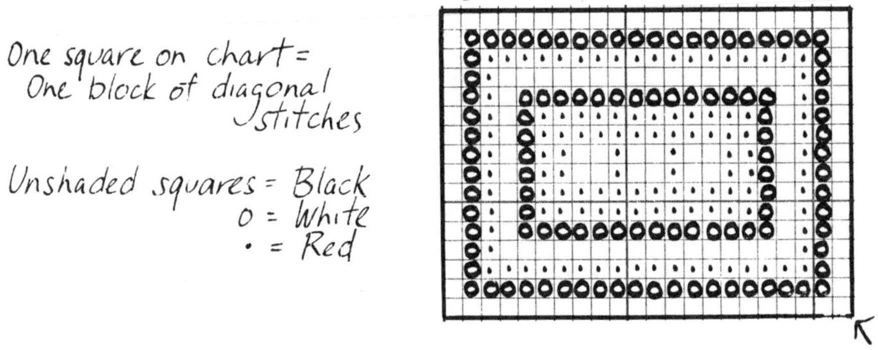

One square on chart =
One block of diagonal
stitches

Unshaded squares = Black
o = White
· = Red

4 . African Designs

The colors and patterns in this chapter may be a totally new departure for you in decorating your home. Based on actual West African fabrics or blankets, the afghans are worked in strips to be joined later, just as the native craftsmen would weave narrow strips of material and then sew them together afterwards. This technique helps to give an authentic look to the designs, which would look too neat and regular if worked all in one piece. Narrow strips of knitting or crochet are also much easier to handle while working than is one large piece, measuring the entire width of an afghan.

The knitted strips are sewn together using a backstitch. The crocheted strips are joined by an oversewing stitch.

The colors used here have been kept as close as possible to the original fabrics, but you can certainly change them to suit your own decorating needs.

Canvas squares can be sewn together to make rugs or wall hangings, or used as they are for pillows or pictures. Any of the charts provided can be used as the basis for making large rugs worked in one piece, with several repeats of the design worked side by side.

The Persian Needlepoint Wool used for most of the canvas work may be changed for a 4-ply-weight yarn. This will reduce costs, and produce an exact match for the yarns used in the afghans. Approximate yardages are given for every item.

COORDINATES IN AFRICAN CHECKERS (Plate 14)

CROCHETED AFGHAN IN AFRICAN CHECKERS* (Photograph 73)

Finished size: Approx. 44″ × 60″

You need: 4-ply acrylic or knitting worsted yarn
5 4-oz. skeins in Black (shade A)
4 4-oz. skeins in White (shade B)
A size I aluminum crochet hook

Gauge: 6 sts. and 7 rows to 2″ over sc using a size I hook

The Afghan: Figure 121 shows how the finished strips are sewn together to complete the afghan.

Strip #1 (make 3)   With shade A, ch 25.

ROW 1: 1 dc in 4th ch from hook, and 1 dc in each ch across, ch 3, turn.

ROW 2: 1 dc in each dc across, ch 3, turn.
Repeat Row 2 until 8 rows of dc have been worked, join shade B, ch 1, turn.
Work 2 rows in sc in shade B.
Work 2 rows in sc in shade A.

Photo 73: *Crocheted Afghan in African Checkers*

Work 8 rows in dc in shade B.
Work 2 rows in sc in shade A.
Work 2 rows in sc in shade B.
Work 8 rows in dc in shade A.
Work 2 rows in sc in shade B.
Work 2 rows in sc in shade A.
Work 8 rows in dc in shade B.
Work 8 rows in dc in shade A.
Work 2 rows in sc in shade B.
Work 2 rows in sc in shade A.
Work 8 rows in dc in shade B.
Work 2 rows in sc in shade A.
Work 2 rows in sc in shade B.
Work 8 rows in dc in shade A.
Work 2 rows in sc in shade B.
Work 2 rows in sc in shade A.
Work 8 rows in dc in shade B.
Work 2 rows in sc in shade A.
Work 2 rows in sc in shade B.
Work 8 rows in dc in shade A.
Work 8 rows in dc in shade B.
Work 2 rows in sc in shade A.
Work 2 rows in sc in shade B.
Work 8 rows in dc in shade A.
Work 2 rows in sc in shade B.
Work 2 rows in sc in shade A.
Fasten off.

Strip #2 (make 3)   Work exactly as for Strip #1, reversing the colors.

TO FINISH: Sew the strips together as shown in Figure 121, keeping all the foundation chains at the bottom of the work.

EDGING: With shade A and a size I hook, join yarn at bottom left-hand corner about 1″ along lower edge.
Work 1 sc in each foundation ch to next corner, 3 sc in corner to turn.
Work 1 sc in sides of rows up to next corner, 3 sc in corner to turn.
Work 1 sc in each sc across top to next corner, 3 sc in corner to turn.
Work 1 sc in sides of rows down to next corner, 3 sc in corner to turn. Work along foundation chain in sc until the first stitch is reached, sl st in top of first st, ch 1.

Figure 121

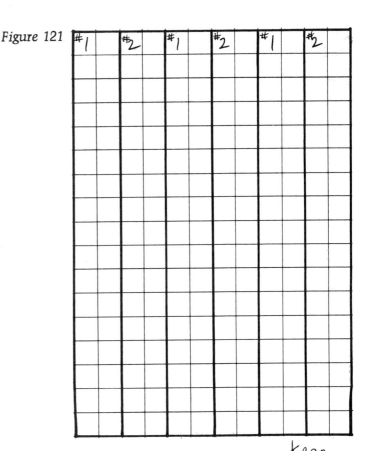

Keep foundation chain of each strip at lower edge when sewing

(not to scale)

KNITTED AFGHAN IN AFRICAN CHECKERS*
(Photograph 74)

Finished size: Approx. 43″ × 54″

You need: 4-ply acrylic or knitting worsted yarn
4 4-oz. skeins in Black (shade A)
4 4-oz. skeins in Red (shade B)
A pair of size 10½ needles
A size I aluminum crochet hook for the
   edging

Gauge: 4 sts. and 5 rows to 1″ over plain st.st. on size 10½
needles

The Afghan: Figure 122 shows how the finished strips are
sewn together to complete the afghan.

Strip #1 (make 3)
With size 10½ needles and shade A, cast on 30 sts.
Work in plain st.st. throughout, and change color as follows:

20 rows in shade A.
2 rows in shade B.
2 rows in shade A.
20 rows in shade B.
2 rows in shade A.
2 rows in shade B.
20 rows in shade A.
2 rows in shade B.
2 rows in shade A.
20 rows in shade B.
20 rows in shade A.
2 rows in shade B.
2 rows in shade A.
20 rows in shade B.
2 rows in shade A.
2 rows in shade B.
20 rows in shade A.

2 rows in shade B.
2 rows in shade A.
20 rows in shade B.

Photo 74:   *Knitted Afghan in
African Checkers*

Figure 122

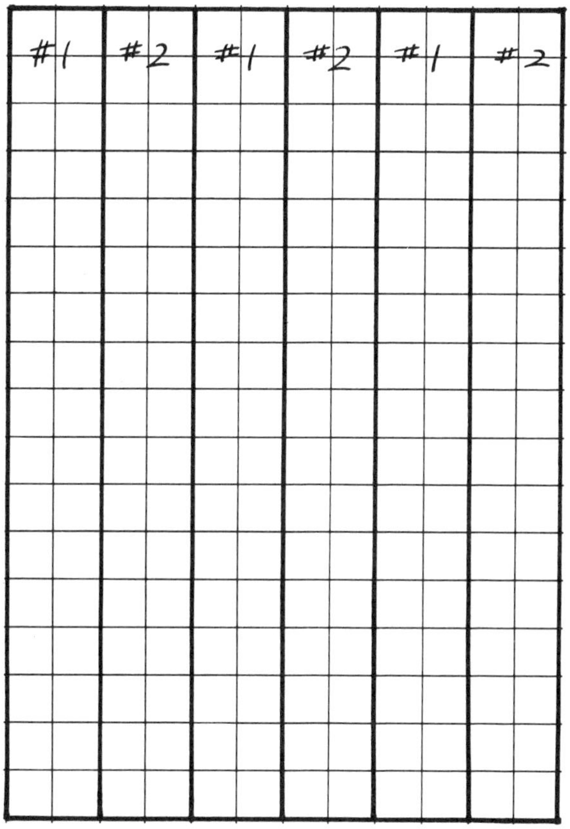

(not to scale)

#1		#2		#1		#2		#1		#2	

2 rows in shade A.
2 rows in shade B.
20 rows in shade A.
20 rows in shade B.
2 rows in shade A.
2 rows in shade B.
20 rows in shade A.
2 rows in shade B.
2 rows in shade A.
Bind off.

Strip #2 (make 3)   Work exactly as for Strip #1, reversing the colors.

Keep cast-on edge at bottom of work when sewing

TO FINISH: Sew the strips together as shown in Figure 122, keeping the lower edge of each strip at the lower edge of the afghan, so that all the knitting is lying in the same direction.

EDGING: With shade B and a size I hook, join yarn at bottom left-hand corner and 1″ along lower edge.
Work 1 sc in the bottom of each knitted stitch to next corner, 3 sc in corner to turn.
Work 1 sc in side of rows up to next corner, 3 sc in corner to turn.
Work 1 sc in top of each knitted stitch to next corner, 3 sc in corner to turn.
Work 1 sc in side of rows down to next corner, 3 sc in corner to turn. Work along bottom of next few stitches until first stitch is reached, sl st in top of first st, ch 1.

ROW 2: Work 1 sc in each sc around, and 3 sc in center st at each corner, join with a sl st to first sc, fasten off.

GOBELIN PILLOW OR PICTURE IN AFRICAN CHECKERS* (Photograph 75)

Finished size: Approx. 14″ × 14″

You need: Persian Needlepoint Wool in 10-yd. skeins.
Black: 8 (80 yds.)
White: 7 (70 yds.)
A piece of 10-mesh-to-1″ mono canvas measuring 18″ × 18″
A number 18 tapestry needle

Method:

1. The entire design is worked over 4 meshes of the canvas in Upright Gobelin Stitch.

2. Start in the lower right-hand corner, at a point 2″ up from bottom and in from side edge.

3. Following the chart in Figure 123, begin work where indicated by the arrow. Work in rows across, until entire chart is completed.

One square on chart = 4 stitches and 4 meshes on canvas

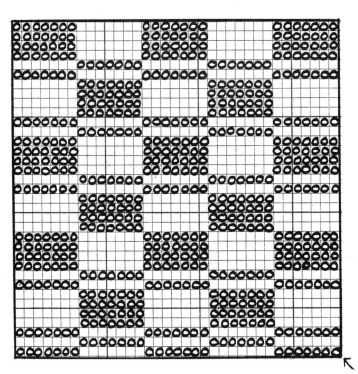

Figure 123

Unshaded squares = White
0 = Black

*Photo 75: Gobelin Pillow or
Picture in African Checkers*

PLACE MAT IN AFRICAN CHECKERS*
(Photograph 76)

Finished size: Approx. 12½″ × 10¼″

You need: Persian Needlepoint Wool in 10-yd. skeins.
Black: 5 (50 yds.)
White: 4 (40 yds.)
A rectangular piece of plastic canvas with 7 holes to 1″, measuring 13¼″ × 10½″
A number 18 tapestry needle

Figure 124

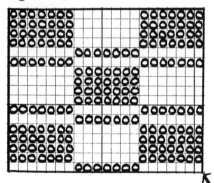

One square on chart =
One block of diagonal stitches

Unshaded squares = White
o = Black

Method:

1. The entire design is worked in blocks of the Diagonal Stitch shown in Chapter 1.

2. One square on the chart shown in Figure 124 is equivalent to 1 completed block of diagonal stitches.

3. Start in the lower right-hand corner, making sure that you work right up to the edge of the canvas (Figure 11). This will reduce the amount of trimming required at the end of work.

4. Following the chart in Figure 124, begin work where indicated by the arrow. Work in rows of blocks across, until entire chart is completed.

5. Trim away excess plastic as shown in Photograph 1.

6. Choose 1 of the colors in the design for the stitched edging. Work in an oversewing stitch from left to right as shown in Figure 12 and described in Chapter 1.

7. *Do not press.*

Photo 76: *Place Mat in African Checkers*

AFRICAN BLANKET COORDINATES (Plate 15)

KNITTED AFGHAN IN AFRICAN BLANKET DESIGN* (Photograph 77)

Finished size: Approx. 42″ × 52″

You need: 4-ply acrylic or knitting worsted yarn
3 4-oz. skeins in Beige (shade A)
3 4-oz. skeins in Brown (shade B)
2 4-oz. skeins in Red (shade C)
A pair of size 10 ½ needles
A size I aluminum crocket hook for edging

Gauge: 4 sts. and 5 rows to 1″ over plain st.st. on size 10½ needles

The Afghan: is worked in 6 identical strips which are afterwards sewn together.

The Strip (make 6)
With size 10½″ needles and shade A, cast on 30 sts.
Work in plain st.st. throughout, and change color as follows:
*4 rows in shade A.
6 rows in shade B.
4 rows in shade A.
2 rows in shade B.
Work 2A, 2B across for 2 rows.
2 rows in shade C.
Work 2A, 2B across for 2 rows.
2 rows in shade B.
4 rows in shade A.
2 rows in shade B.
6 rows in shade C.
2 rows in shade B**
Repeat stripes from * to ** until work measures approx. 54″, finishing with a stripe in shade A. Bind off.

TO FINISH: Sew the strips together along the long edges, keeping the lower edge of each strip at the lower edge of the afghan, so that all the knitting is lying in the same direction.

EDGING: With shade A and a size I hook, join yarn at bottom left-hand corner about 1″ along lower edge.
Work 1 sc in the bottom of each knitted stitch to next corner, 3 sc in corner to turn.

Work 1 sc in side of rows up to next corner, 3 sc in corner to turn.

Work 1 sc in top of each knitted stitch to next corner, 3 sc in corner to turn.

Work 1 sc in side of rows down to next corner, 3 sc in corner to turn.

Work along bottom of next few stitches until first stitch is reached, sl st in top of first st, ch 1.

ROW 2: Work 1 sc in each sc around, and 3 sc in center sc at each corner, join with a sl st to first sc, fasten off.

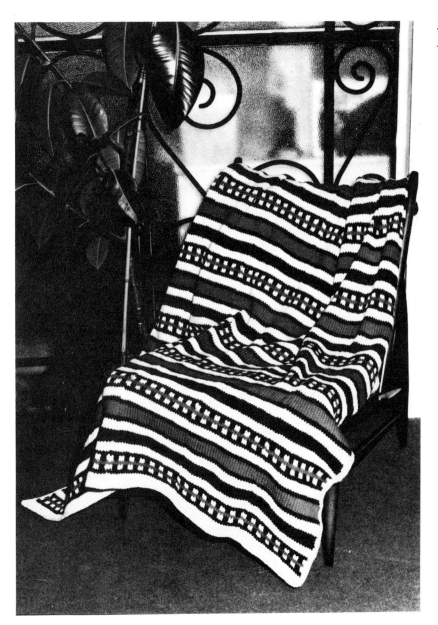

Photo 77: Knitted Afghan in African Blanket Design

GOBELIN PILLOW OR PICTURE IN AFRICAN BLANKET DESIGN* (Photograph 78)

Finished size: Approx. 14″ × 14″

You need: Persian Needlepoint Wool in 10-yd. skeins.
Beige: 8 (80 yds.)
Rust: 8 (80 yds.)
Red: 5 (50 yds.)
A piece of 10-mesh-to-1″ mono canvas measuring 18″ × 18″
A number 18 tapestry needle

Photo 78: Gobelin Pillow or Picture in African Blanket Design

Method:

1. The entire design is worked over 4 meshes of the canvas in Upright Gobelin Stitch.

2. Start in the lower right-hand corner, at a point 2″ up from bottom and in from side edge.

3. Following the chart in Figure 125 begin work where indicated by the arrow. Work in rows across, until entire chart is completed.

Figure 125

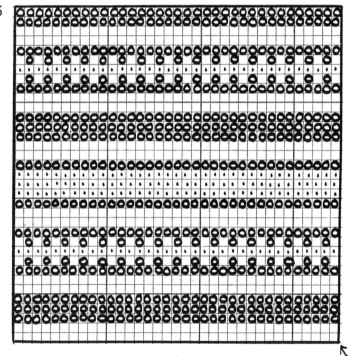

One square on chart = 4 stitches and 4 meshes on canvas

Unshaded squares = Beige
o = Rust
· = Red

COORDINATES IN AFRICAN STRIPES (Plate 16)

CROCHETED AFGHAN IN AFRICAN STRIPES*
(Photograph 79)

Finished size: Approx. 40″ × 60″

You need: 4-ply acrylic or knitting worsted yarn
6 4-oz. skeins in Black (shade A)
1 4-oz. skein in White (shade B)
1 4-oz. skein in Red (shade C)
1 4-oz. skein in Orange (shade D)
1 4-oz. skein in Turquoise (shade E)
A size I aluminum crochet hook

Gauge: 6 sts. and 7 rows to 2″ over sc using a size I hook

Photo 79: *Crocheted Afghan in
African Stripes*

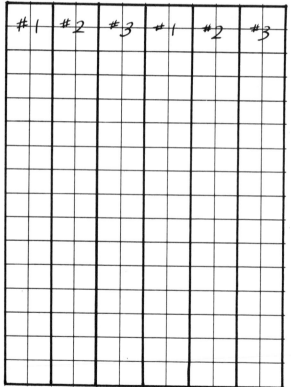

Figure 126

keep foundation chains at lower edge of work
when sewing

The Afghan: Figure 126 shows how the finished strips are sewn together to complete the afghan.

Strip #1 (make 2)
With shade D and a size I hook, ch 22.

ROW 1: Starting in 2nd ch from hook, work 1 sc in each ch across, ch 1, turn.

ROW 2: Work 1 sc in each sc across, change to shade A and continue stripes as follows:

*2 rows in sc in shade A.	2 rows in sc in shade B.
2 rows in sc in shade D.	2 rows in sc in shade A.
6 rows in dc in shade A.	2 rows in sc in shade B.
2 rows in sc in shade B.	2 rows in sc in shade A.
2 rows in sc in shade A.	2 rows in sc in shade B.
2 rows in sc in shade B.	2 rows in sc in shade A.
2 rows in sc in shade A.	2 rows in sc in shade B.
2 rows in sc in shade B.	2 rows in sc in shade E.
6 rows in dc in shade A.	2 rows in sc in shade A.
2 rows in sc in shade D.	2 rows in sc in shade E.
2 rows in sc in shade A.	6 rows in dc in shade A.
2 rows in sc in shade D.	2 rows in sc in shade D.**
6 rows in dc in shade A.	Repeat from * to ** once more.
2 rows in sc in shade E.	2 rows in sc in shade A.
2 rows in sc in shade A.	2 rows in sc in shade D.
2 rows in sc in shade E.	6 rows in dc in shade A, fasten off.

Strip #2 (make 2)
With shade C and size I hook, ch 22.

ROW 1: Starting in 2nd ch from hook, work 1 sc in each ch across, ch 1, turn.

ROW 2: Work 1 sc in each sc across, change to shade A and continue stripes as follows:

*2 rows in sc in shade A.	2 rows in sc in shade C.
2 rows in sc in shade C.	6 rows in dc in shade B.
6 rows in dc in shade A.	2 rows in sc in shade C.
2 rows in sc in shade B.	2 rows in sc in shade A.
2 rows in sc in shade A.	2 rows in sc in shade C.
2 rows in sc in shade B.	6 rows in dc in shade A.
2 rows in sc in shade A.	2 rows in sc in shade C.**
2 rows in sc in shade B.	Repeat from * to ** once more.
6 rows in dc in shade A.	2 rows in sc in shade A.
2 rows in sc in shade C.	2 rows in sc in shade C.
2 rows in sc in shade A.	6 rows in dc in shade A, fasten off.

Strip #3 (make 2)
With shade C and a size I hook, ch 22.

ROW 1: Starting in 2nd ch from hook, work 1 sc in each ch across, ch 1, turn.

ROW 2: Work 1 sc in each sc across, change to shade A and continue stripes as follows:

*2 rows in sc in shade A.   2 rows in sc in shade B.
2 rows in sc in shade C.   2 rows in sc in shade A.
6 rows in dc in shade A.   2 rows in sc in shade B.
2 rows in sc in shade B.   2 rows in sc in shade A.
2 rows in sc in shade A.   2 rows in sc in shade B.
2 rows in sc in shade B.   2 rows in sc in shade A.
2 rows in sc in shade A.   2 rows in sc in shade B.
2 rows in sc in shade B.   2 rows in sc in shade C.
6 rows in dc in shade A.   2 rows in sc in shade A.
2 rows in sc in shade D.   2 rows in sc in shade C.
2 rows in sc in shade A.   6 rows in dc in shade A.
2 rows in sc in shade D.   2 rows in sc in shade C**
6 rows in dc in shade A.   Repeat from * to ** once more.
2 rows in sc in shade C.   2 rows in sc in shade A.
2 rows in sc in shade A.   2 rows in sc in shade C.
2 rows in sc in shade C.   6 rows in dc in shade A, fasten off.

TO FINISH: Sew the strips together as shown in Figure 126, keeping all the foundation chains at the bottom of the work.

EDGING: With shade A and a size I hook, join yarn at bottom left-hand corner about 1" along lower edge.
Work 1 sc in each foundation ch to next corner, 3 sc in corner to turn.
Work 1 sc in sides of rows up to next corner, 3 sc in corner to turn.
Work 1 sc in each sc across top to next corner, 3 sc in corner to turn.
Work 1 sc in sides of rows down to next corner, 3 sc in corner to turn.
Work along foundation chain in sc until the first stitch is reached, sl st in top of first st, ch 1.

ROW 2: Work 1 sc in each sc around, and 3 sc in center st at each corner, join with a sl st to first sc, fasten off.

GOBELIN PILLOW OR PICTURE IN AFRICAN STRIPES* (Photograph 80)

Finished size: Approx. 14″ × 14″

You need: Persian Needlepoint Wool in 10-yd. skeins
Black: 8 (80 yds.)
White: 3 (30 yds.)
Red: 2 (20 yds.)
Turquoise: 1 (10 yds.)
Orange: 1 (10 yds.)
A piece of 10-mesh-to-1″ mono canvas measuring 18″ × 18″
A number 18 tapestry needle

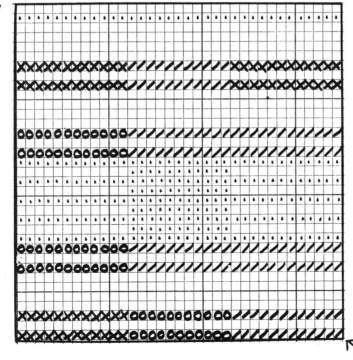

Photo 80: *Gobelin Pillow or Picture in African Stripes*

Method:

1. The entire design is worked over 4 meshes of the canvas in Upright Gobelin Stitch.

2. Start in the lower right-hand corner, at a point 2″ up from bottom and in from side edge.

3. Following the chart in Figure 127, begin work where indicated by the arrow. Work in rows across, until entire chart is completed.

Figure 127

One square on chart =
4 stitches and 4 meshes
on canvas

Unshaded squares = Black
O = Turquoise
• = White
X = Orange
/ = Red

TABLE MAT IN AFRICAN STRIPES*
(Photograph 81)

Finished size: Approx. 12 ½″ × 10 ¼″

You need: Persian Needlepoint Wool in 10-yd. skeins.
Black: 4 (40 yds.)
White: 3 (30 yds.)
Red: 2 (20 yds.)
Turquoise: 1 (10 yds.)
A rectangular piece of plastic canvas with 7 holes to 1″, measuring 13 ¼″ × 10 ½″
A number 18 tapestry needle

Method:

1. The entire design is worked in blocks of the Diagonal Stitch shown in Chapter 1.

2. One square on the chart shown in Figure 128 is equivalent to 1 completed block of diagonal stitches.

3. Start in the lower right-hand corner, making sure that you work right up to the edge of the canvas (Figure 11). This will reduce the amount of trimming required at the end of work.

4. Following the chart in Figure 128, begin work where indicated by the arrow. Work in rows of blocks across, until entire chart is completed.

5. Trim away excess plastic as shown in Photograph 1.

6. Choose 1 of the colors in the design for the stitched edging. Work in an oversewing stitch from left to right as shown in Figure 12, and described in Chapter 1.

7. *Do not press.*

Photo 81: *Table Mat in African Stripes*

One square on chart =
One block of diagonal
stitches

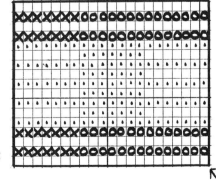

Figure 128

Unshaded squares = Black
X = Turquoise
· = White
o = Red

COORDINATES IN AFRICAN PATTERNS (Plate 17)

GOBELIN PILLOW OR PICTURE IN BRILLIANT PATTERNS** (Photograph 82)

Finished size: Approx. 14″ × 14″

You need: Persian Needlepoint Wool in 10-yd. skeins.
Black: 8 (80 yds.)
White: 6 (60 yds.)
Red: 2 (20 yds.)
Orange: 1 (10 yds.)
Turquoise: 1 (10 yds.)
A piece of 10-mesh-to-1″ mono canvas measuring 18″ × 18″
A number 18 tapestry needle

Method:

1. The entire design is worked over 2 meshes of the canvas in Upright Gobelin Stitch. Advice on how to work this stitch is given in Chapter 1.

Photo 82:   Gobelin Pillow or Picture in Brilliant Patterns

One square on chart = 2 stitches and 2 meshes on canvas

Figure 129

Unshaded squares = Black
O = White
• = Red
/ = Orange
X = Turquoise

2. Start in the lower right-hand corner, at a point 2″ up from bottom and in from side edge.

3. Following the chart in Figure 129, begin work where indicated by the arrow. Work in rows across, until entire chart is completed.

GOBELIN PILLOW OR PICTURE IN AFRICAN STRIPS** (Photograph 83)

Finished size: Approx. 14″ × 14″

You need: Persian Needlepoint Wool in 10-yd. skeins.
White: 9 (90 yds.)
Black: 6 (60 yds.)
Red: 2 (20 yds.)
A piece of 10-mesh-to-1″ mono canvas measuring 18″ × 18″
A number 18 tapestry needle

Photo 83: *Gobelin Pillow or Picture in African Stripes*

One square on chart = 2 stitches and 2 meshes on canvas

Figure 130

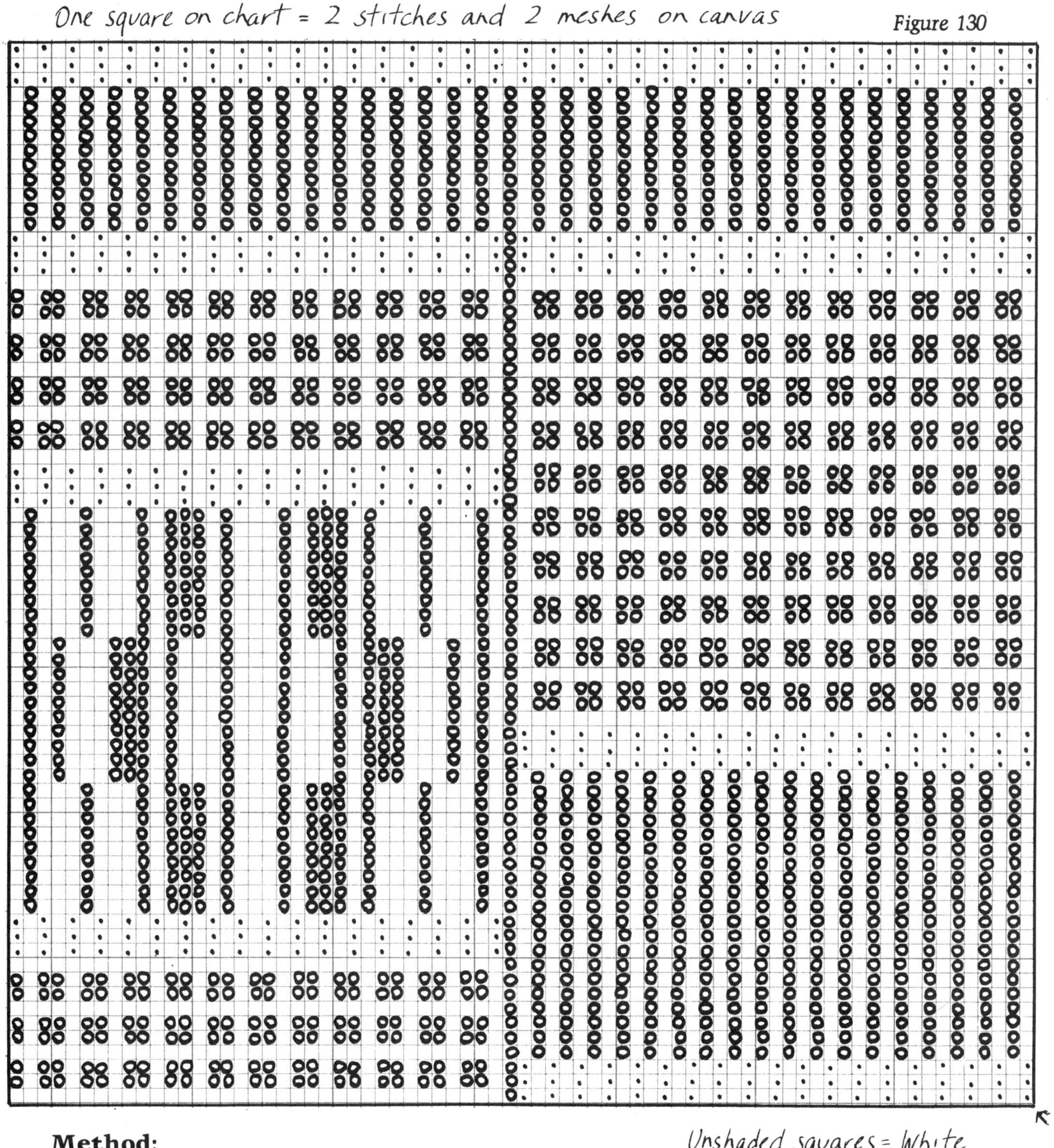

Unshaded squares = White
0 = Black
• = Red

Method:

1. The entire design is worked over 2 meshes of the canvas in Upright Gobelin Stitch. Advice on how to work this stitch is given in Chapter 1.

2. Start in the lower right-hand corner, at a point 2″ up from bottom and in from side edge.

3. Following the chart in Figure 130, begin work where indicated by the arrow. Work in rows across, until entire chart is completed.

AFRICAN TABLE MAT # 1 (Photograph 84)

Finished size: Approx. 13 ¼″ × 10 ¼″

You need: Persian Needlepoint Wool in 10-yd. skeins.
White: 5 (50 yds.)
Black: 3 (30 yds.)
Red: 2 (20 yds.)
A rectangular piece of plastic canvas with 7 holes to 1″, measuring 13 ¼″ × 10½″
A number 18 tapestry needle

Method:

1. The entire design is worked in blocks of the Diagonal Stitch shown in Chapter 1.

2. One square on the chart shown in Figure 131 is equivalent to 1 completed block of diagonal stitches.

3. Start in the lower right-hand corner, making sure that you work right up to the edge of the canvas (Figure 11). This will reduce the amount of trimming required at the end of work.

4. Following the chart in Figure 131, begin work where indicated by the arrow. Work in rows of blocks across, until entire chart is completed.

5. Trim away excess plastic as shown in Photograph 1.

6. Choose 1 of the colors in the design for the stitched edging. Work in an oversewing stitch from left to right as shown in Figure 12 and described in Chapter 1.

7. *Do not press.*

Photo 84: *African Table Mat #1*

One square on chart =
One block of
diagonal stitches

Unshaded squares = White
O = Black
• = Red

Figure 131

AFRICAN TABLE MAT # 2 *(Photograph 85)*

Finished size: Approx. 12 ½" × 10 ¼"

You need: Persian Needlepoint Wool in 10-yd. skeins.
White: 5 (50 yds.)
Red: 4 (40 yds.)
Black: 1 (10 yds.)
A rectangular piece of plastic canvas with 7 holes to 1" measuring 13 ¼" × 10 ½"
A number 18 tapestry needle

Method:

1. The entire design is worked in blocks of the Diagonal Stitch shown in Chapter 1.

2. One square on the chart shown in Figure 132 is equivalent to 1 completed block of diagonal stitches.

3. Start in the lower right-hand corner, making sure that you work right up to the edge of the canvas (Figure 11). This will reduce the amount of trimming required at the end of work.

4. Following the chart in Figure 132, begin work where indicated by the arrow. Work in rows of blocks across, until entire chart is completed.

5. Trim away excess plastic as shown in Photograph 1.

6. Choose 1 of the colors in the design for the stitched edging. Work in an oversewing stitch from left to right as shown in Figure 12, and described in Chapter 1.

7. *Do not press.*

Figure 132

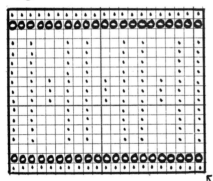

One square on chart = One block of diagonal stitches

Unshaded squares = White
0 = Black
• = Red

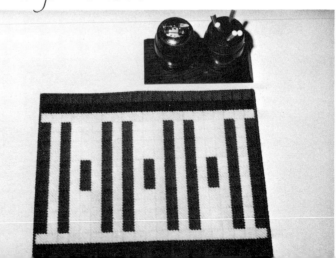

Photo 85:   *African Table Mat #2*